THE HISTORY OF THE
AMERICAN GUITAR
FROM 1833 TO THE PRESENT DAY

BY TONY BACON

FRIEDMAN/FAIRFAX
PUBLISHERS

THE HISTORY OF THE AMERICAN GUITAR
BY TONY BACON

Copyright © 2001 Outline Press Ltd
Text copyright © Tony Bacon
All rights reserved

A FRIEDMAN/FAIRFAX BOOK
Friedman/Fairfax Publishers

Please visit our website: www.metrobooks.com

© 2001 by Friedman/Fairfax Publishers.

This edition published by Friedman/Fairfax
by arrangement with Balafon Books, an imprint of Outline Press Limited

ISBN 1-58663-297-3

3 5 7 9 10 8 6 4 2

Distributed by Sterling Publishing Company, Inc.
387 Park Avenue South
New York, NY 10016

Distributed in Canada by Sterling Publishing
Canadian Manda Group
One Atlantic Avenue, Suite 105
Toronto, Ontario, Canada M6K 3E7

Distributed in Australia by
Capricorn Link (Australia) Pty Ltd.
P.O. Box 6651
Baulkham Hills, Business Centre, NSW 2153, Australia

Art Director: Nigel Osborne
Design: Sally Stockwell
Photography: Miki Slingsby
Editor: Paul Quinn

Origination by Global Colour, Malaysia
Print by Tien Wah Press Limited, Singapore

CONTENTS

INTRODUCTION

Many theories have been offered to account for the birth of the guitar. Some place the event in Asia, others in Africa, or in Europe. It happened hundreds and hundreds of years ago. No one agrees on the precise details, and nor is it likely that anyone ever will. Much more certain is that the most important early contribution to the history of the American guitar was made by the German immigrant Christian Frederick Martin.

That is where this book's story begins. During the course of the pages that follow, all manner of characters, inventors, players and mavericks will appear, turning the course of the guitar first this way, then that. Guitar players have always wanted more from the instruments that serve them: a little more volume and power, perhaps; an extra string or two here, maybe; some wild new pickups and a wang-bar bolted on the end; a contraption inside that just might make this particular picker sound better than anyone else.

We map here the American guitar's successes and calamities, the great names and the lesser known heroes, the true geniuses and the failed charlatans. We take you year by year through the key events, and present wonderful pictures of stunning instruments, with a text to match the unfolding story. And it all begins with Mr. Martin in New York in the 1830s... At first, Martin made "flat-top" guitars in the style of his German mentor, Johann Georg Stauffer. The banjo was still the most popular stringed instrument in America at this time, and Martin's belief in the guitar had to wait some years before popular demand caught up.

In the early years of the 20th century some American guitar makers began to use steel strings rather than the traditional gut types. Orville Gibson was one such visionary. He had moved from New York State to Kalamazoo, Michigan, probably around 1880, and started making archtop mandolins and guitars there in the mid 1890s. The now-famous Gibson company was formed in 1902 when Orville teamed up with some businessmen, but he soon left the operation.

Carl Larson and his brother August, based in Chicago, also recognized that guitarists had to be heard alongside loud banjos and mandolins, and used steel strings on their guitars from an early date. Martin made the move during the 1920s to steel strings, offering them on all Martin models by the end of the decade. At the same time, Martin began to modify the size of the guitar, and in the 1910s hit on the important "dreadnought" guitar design. The thick waist and wide, squared shoulders of the large dreadnought body increased still further the flat-top's volume, power and tonal versatility.

Meanwhile at Gibson a new type of steel-string acoustic guitar was in development: the archtop. Lloyd Loar's Master Series L-5 of 1922 defined the genre, apparently having more in common with a violin than a guitar. It had a carved arched top, two f-holes instead of a single round soundhole, a floating height-adjustable bridge with strings fastened to a separate metal tailpiece, and a neck-strengthening truss-rod. Most of this was again designed to create fine tone and to improve sound projection. Other archtop makers would follow, including D'Angelico, Stromberg and, later, D'Aquisto and Benedetto.

Resonator guitars were introduced by National in Los Angeles in 1927. This attempt to provide a louder guitar was more unconventional: inside a metal body, three metal resonator discs were mounted underneath the bridge, acting like mechanical loudspeakers to thrust forward the brash sound of the guitar. The result was relatively crude but effective, and created a new, different sound.

But it was becoming clear that the limits of what could be achieved with a purely acoustic instrument were being reached. The answer was clear to some: electric amplification. A number of players and guitar-makers began to experiment during the 1920s and 1930s, and in 1931 an experimental one-off instrument, the wooden Rickenbacker "Frying Pan" guitar, became the first guitar to feature an electro-magnetic pickup – and was thus the basis for virtually all modern electric guitars.

A number of other US makers began to add magnetic pickups to existing acoustic guitars, but also started to develop models that were built entirely as electric instruments. At first these were primarily in the archtop style and were produced by companies such as National, Rickenbacker, Epiphone and Gibson. The pickups and associated amplifiers were crude. Before World War II, little interest was generated among musicians for the new electric guitar, but after the war the instrument began to make its mark. Soon every manufacturer of note was producing electric models and players increasingly used them in the new styles of popular music that were beginning to emerge.

Another significant development was the solidbody electric guitar, with Fender leading the way in the 1950s. Again, all manner of instruments have followed in this style, with PRS one of the most notable modern makers. Also in recent years there have been interesting hybrids from companies such as Parker that exploit the combination of traditional magnetic pickups with more "acoustic-sounding" piezo pickups, first developed by Ovation. Flat-tops have been repopularized through a number of crazes for acoustic instruments, and manufacturers such as Taylor and Collings are leading the way – with the modern Martin operation still very much in evidence, some 170 years since its founder first set up shop in his newly adopted country.

Virtually all the guitars displayed in these pages come from the fabulous collection assembled by the late Scott Chinery, and this book is dedicated to the memory of Scott and his unmatched determination to celebrate the invention and artistry of the great American guitar makers. Still the guitar adapts to new musical surroundings amid the constant pressure from players to provide that little bit extra at each performance. This book shows how we arrived at today's wonderful diversity of instruments, and points the way to an even more fascinating future.

▲ **(Attributed to) STAUFFER**

PRODUCED: *Austria, early 1800s*

THIS EXAMPLE: *c1820s*

BODY: *11½" wide, 3½" deep*

Johann Georg Stauffer was born in Vienna in the late 1770s, and became one of Austria's most notable makers of guitars.

▼ **MARTIN STAUFFER-STYLE**

PRODUCED: *c1833-1840s*

THIS EXAMPLE: *c1833; serial 1173*

BODY: *12⅝" wide, 4¼" deep*

The dawning of the American guitar starts here with this instrument, custom made by C. F. Martin in New York in the early 1830s for someone called Theresa Rand. Martin brought to America European ideas, directly influenced by Johann Stauffer, an Austrian guitar maker with whom Christian Martin had worked during the 1820s. As the story progresses through the many pages that follow, you will be able to observe the development of the modern guitar as it unfolds before you – and along the way view some fine examples of the art of American guitar making.

1833

*C. F. MARTIN ARRIVES
IN THE USA*

Martin's first American guitars were lookalikes based on the work of Austrian maker Johann Stauffer, with whom Martin had been apprenticed in the 1820s.

▼ **MARTIN STAUFFER-STYLE**

PRODUCED: *c1833-1840s*

THIS EXAMPLE: *c1830s; serial 1114*

BODY: *11½" wide, 3¼" deep*

The guitars that C. F. Martin made in his first years in America were very similar to those of Johann Stauffer, the Austrian guitar maker. Later, of course, Martin began to refine and develop his own ideas as he worked in his newly adopted country. But it's worth comparing the design similarities of this ornate Stauffer-style Martin (and the example shown above) and the two Stauffer-attributed guitars pictured at the top of these pages.

▼ (Attributed to) STAUFFER

PRODUCED: *Austria, early 1800s*

THIS EXAMPLE: *c1820s*

BODY: *11½" wide, 3¼" deep*

C. F. Martin worked for Stauffer in the early

1820s, and while he was there Martin learned much about the construction and design of guitars. Compare, for example, the angled fingerboard design of this guitar (its beautifully figured back is shown below) with that of the Martin at the bottom of the opposite page.

▼ MARTIN

THIS EXAMPLE: *c1840s*

BODY: *11" wide, 4" deep*

Gradually, Christian Martin began to bring to the guitars he made more of his own ideas on construction and design. The most obvious visual change when comparing this example to the earlier Stauffer-style is the narrower upper body, giving an overall shape that is more like a modern guitar.

Christian Frederick Martin, a German immigrant, arrived in the United States in September 1833. In a few decades he would change the course of American guitar making, setting the general style, construction and design of the instrument, and eventually helping to establish the idea that the guitar could be an important musical instrument.

In the 1820s Martin had been a foreman at the Vienna workshop of the innovative Austrian guitar maker Johann Stauffer, but some years before he made his trip across the Atlantic Martin had moved back home to Germany and tried to set up a guitar- and violin-making business there.

A dispute with local instrument makers dragged on and frustrated the evidently ambitious Martin, and led him to leave Europe and try his luck in America, a wide open land of

opportunity. In his new home of New York City, C. F. Martin set up a music store where he sold all kinds of instruments and accessories. Beyond the daily business that allowed him to make a living, Martin also began to make guitars, of which in the first few years he would sell maybe one a week. These earliest of Martin guitars were very much in the style of Martin's old Austrian mentor, Stauffer, with small, hourglass-shape bodies and distinctive scrolled pegheads that had tuning machines in a curving row along one side.

The banjo was the most fashionable stringed instrument of the time in America, strengthened by the popularity of minstrel shows from the 1840s. Martin's belief in the viability of the guitar would have to wait a number of years before popular demand caught up with his ideas.

1839

MARTIN MOVES TO PENNSYLVANIA

This year C. F. Martin and his family move from New York – where they had first settled upon arrival in America six years earlier – to the more rural setting of Cherry Hill, Pennsylvania. (The Martin company continues to operate from this area today.) After the move west, Martin does not want to lose the business he has built up in New York. So he maintains dealings there with the help of a number of guitar teachers and distributors based in the city, including John Coupa, Charles Bruno and the C. A. Zoebisch company.

▼ MARTIN & SCHATZ

PRODUCED: *c1840*

THIS EXAMPLE: *c1840; serial 1296*

BODY: *11½″ wide, 3½″ deep*

Henry Schatz was a German friend of C. F. Martin who moved to America just before Martin. In their new home, Schatz had instruments built for him by Martin, including this example.

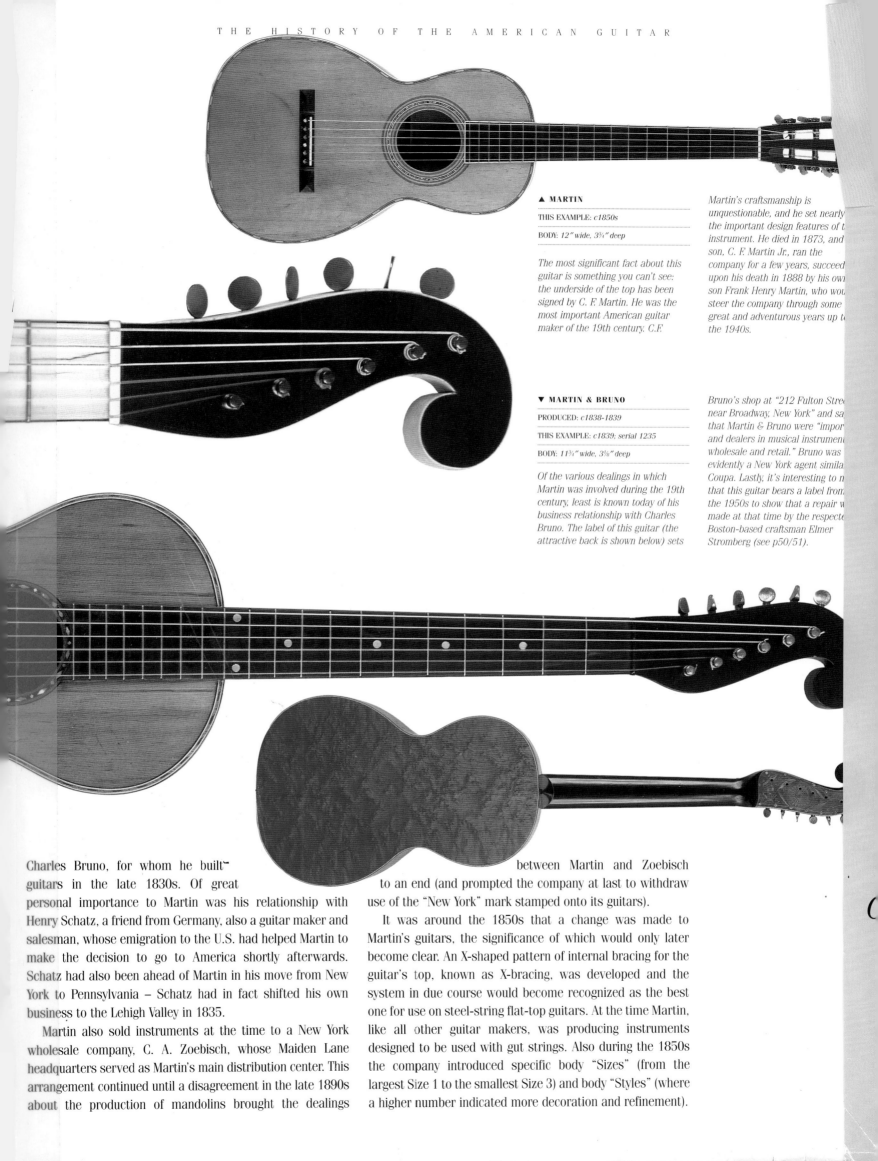

▲ **MARTIN**

THIS EXAMPLE: *c1850s*

BODY: *12″ wide, 3¾″ deep*

The most significant fact about this guitar is something you can't see: the underside of the top has been signed by C. F. Martin. He was the most important American guitar maker of the 19th century. C.F.

Martin's craftsmanship is unquestionable, and he set nearly the important design features of t instrument. He died in 1873, and son, C. F. Martin Jr., ran the company for a few years, succeede upon his death in 1888 by his ow son Frank Henry Martin, who wou steer the company through some great and adventurous years up t the 1940s.

▼ **MARTIN & BRUNO**

PRODUCED: *c1838-1839*

THIS EXAMPLE: *c1839; serial 1235*

BODY: *11¾″ wide, 3⅛″ deep*

Of the various dealings in which Martin was involved during the 19th century, least is known today of his business relationship with Charles Bruno. The label of this guitar (the attractive back is shown below) sets

Bruno's shop at "212 Fulton Stree near Broadway, New York" and sa that Martin & Bruno were "impor and dealers in musical instrument wholesale and retail." Bruno was evidently a New York agent simila Coupa. Lastly, it's interesting to n that this guitar bears a label from the 1950s to show that a repair w made at that time by the respecte Boston-based craftsman Elmer Stromberg (see p50/51).

Charles Bruno, for whom he built guitars in the late 1830s. Of great personal importance to Martin was his relationship with Henry Schatz, a friend from Germany, also a guitar maker and salesman, whose emigration to the U.S. had helped Martin to make the decision to go to America shortly afterwards. Schatz had also been ahead of Martin in his move from New York to Pennsylvania – Schatz had in fact shifted his own business to the Lehigh Valley in 1835.

Martin also sold instruments at the time to a New York wholesale company, C. A. Zoebisch, whose Maiden Lane headquarters served as Martin's main distribution center. This arrangement continued until a disagreement in the late 1890s about the production of mandolins brought the dealings between Martin and Zoebisch to an end (and prompted the company at last to withdraw use of the "New York" mark stamped onto its guitars).

It was around the 1850s that a change was made to Martin's guitars, the significance of which would only later become clear. An X-shaped pattern of internal bracing for the guitar's top, known as X-bracing, was developed and the system in due course would become recognized as the best one for use on steel-string flat-top guitars. At the time Martin, like all other guitar makers, was producing instruments designed to be used with gut strings. Also during the 1850s the company introduced specific body "Sizes" (from the largest Size 1 to the smallest Size 3) and body "Styles" (where a higher number indicated more decoration and refinement).

c.1883

LYON & HEALY MAKES THE FIRST WASHBURN GUITARS

Built at various times by manufacturers such as Lyon & Healy, J. R. Stewart, Gibson and Regal, Washburn guitars reveal an intriguing story.

Toward the end of the 19th century, Chicago had become the center of the musical instrument industry in the United States. One of the biggest operators there was Lyon & Healy, founded in 1864 by Boston music dealer Oliver Ditson as his Chicago branch and named for Ditson's associates who ran it, George Washburn Lyon and Patrick J. Healy.

By 1880 Lyon & Healy was independent of Ditson and had become the largest music retailer in the Midwest. It was around this time that Lyon & Healy started selling fretted instruments marked with the George Washburn brand.

Until relatively recently, in fact, "Washburn" has never been a company, but rather a brandname applied to instruments manufactured and sold by a variety of companies. George W. Lyon retired from Lyon & Healy in 1889, after which time the

Washburn line in particular and Lyon & Healy's fretted instrument production in general seem to have blossomed. Patrick Healy evidently decided that the time was right to build a modern factory, to mass-produce guitars, banjos, mandolins and zithers, and to flood the market.

Guitar historian Mike Newton, source of much of the Washburn material here, says: "A Washburn of this time might not have had the craftsmanship of a Martin, but the line had something for everyone in every price range. It's no exaggeration to say that Patrick Healy was one of the true fathers of the American guitar industry." Healy's vision proved to be faultless, and for the next 25 years Lyon & Healy

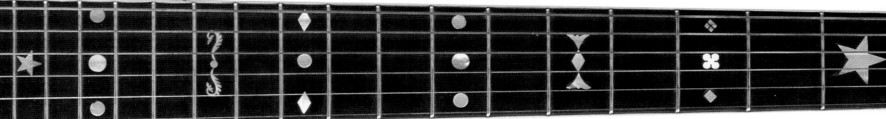

▼ WASHBURN STYLE 108

PRODUCED: *c1889-1896*

THIS EXAMPLE: *c1892; serial 46341*

BODY: *12⅝″ wide, 3¾″ deep*

This is a beautiful example of the kind of guitars Lyon & Healy were making in Chicago at the end of the 19th century. The back seam inside the body is stamped "George Washburn," the brand named for

George Washburn Lyon who co-founded Lyon & Healy in 1864. At the time Style 108 was sold, the first number of the Style indicated body size (1 here indicates Washburn's Standard size; there were four other sizes), and the last number stood for decoration, with 9 the highest. This pearl-laden 108 retailed for $80, compared to the $70 that Martin was asking for its much less fancy model 1-42 around the same time.

▶ WASHBURN "BELL" STYLE 5271

PRODUCED: *c1925-1929*

THIS EXAMPLE: *c1929; serial 9122/1697*

BODY: *15½″ wide, 3½″ deep*

The unusual shape of the shortlived Bell guitar was intended to provide a new tonal character. Lyon & Healy's catalog said that the $195 Bell was designed for the player "who feels that he must have the very best guitar that money can buy."

▲ HAYNES

PRODUCED: *c1865-1897*

THIS EXAMPLE: *c1870*

BODY: *12″ wide, 3¼″ deep*

John C. Haynes of Boston made instruments like this one in his own right, as well as working for the Ditson company. This guitar features William B. Tilton's "Improvement," a metal disc mounted in the soundhole supposed to add to the tonality of the instrument, but it seems to be more of a gimmick than of any useful substance.

flourished, making everything from cheap student instruments to elaborate pearl-encrusted Washburns. But by the 1920s competition had grown, business was down, and most of the elaborate Washburn models had been dropped from the company's lines.

"By 1925 Washburns were plainer than Martins, not as good, and they cost more," notes Newton. The cheap "student" lines were gone, and Lyon & Healy no longer distributed Washburns themselves, having shifted that work to Tonk Bros., a Chicago-based "jobber" (a wholesaler who sells a variety of items to retail stores from different sources). In 1928 Lyon & Healy finally got

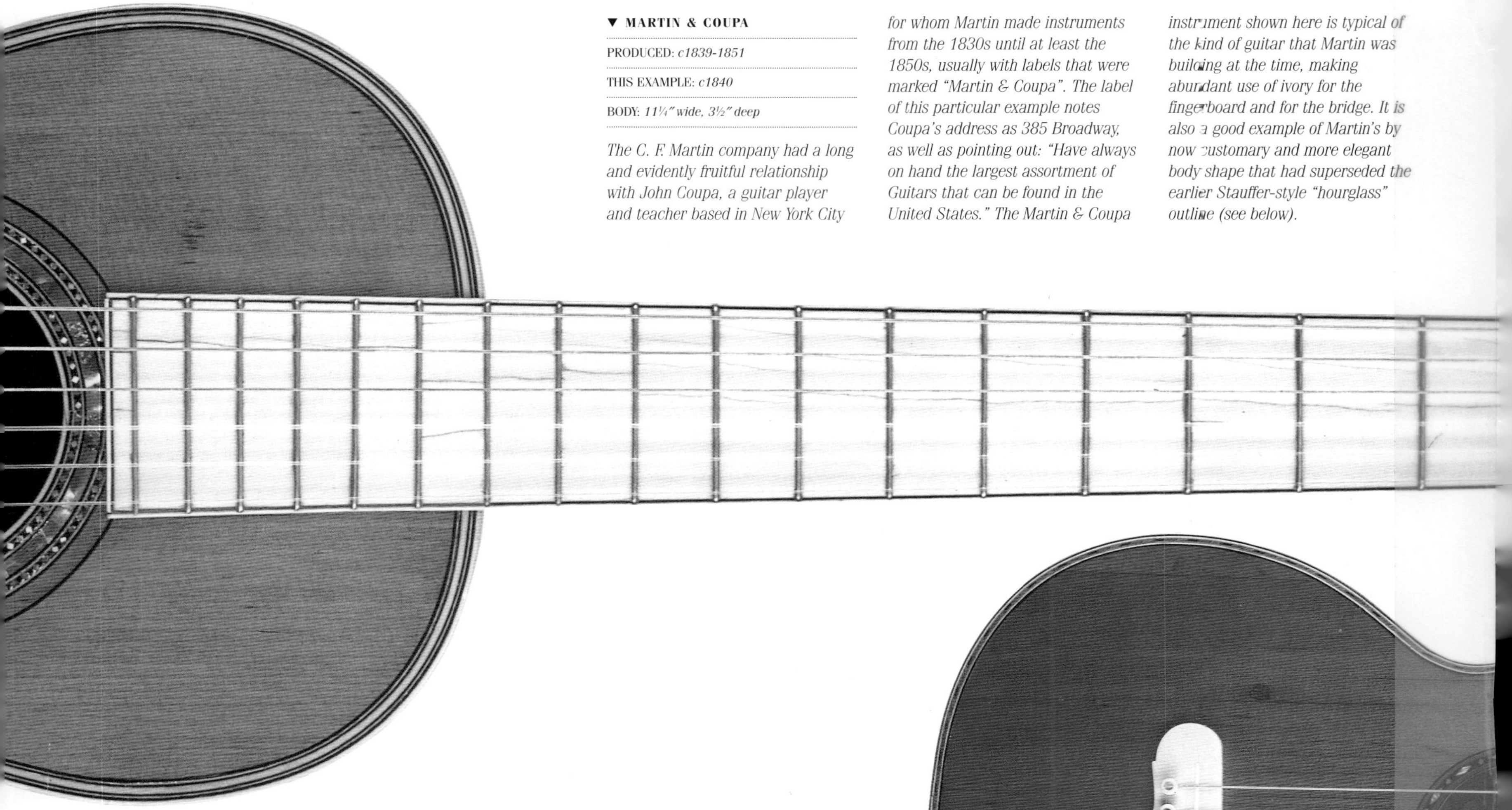

▼ MARTIN & COUPA

PRODUCED: *c1839-1851*

THIS EXAMPLE: *c1840*

BODY: *11¼" wide, 3½" deep*

The C. F. Martin company had a long and evidently fruitful relationship with John Coupa, a guitar player and teacher based in New York City

for whom Martin made instruments from the 1830s until at least the 1850s, usually with labels that were marked "Martin & Coupa". The label of this particular example notes Coupa's address as 385 Broadway, as well as pointing out: "Have always on hand the largest assortment of Guitars that can be found in the United States." The Martin & Coupa

instrument shown here is typical of the kind of guitar that Martin was building at the time, making abundant use of ivory for the fingerboard and for the bridge. It is also a good example of Martin's by now customary and more elegant body shape that had superseded the earlier Stauffer-style "hourglass" outline (see below).

▼ MARTIN

THIS EXAMPLE: *c1850s*

BODY: *12" wide, 4" deep*

This may be the first X-braced steel-string guitar Martin made, and is therefore one of the most important

Martin instruments illustrated in this book. It's interesting to speculate how music might have developed in a totally different way had Martin not come up with the X-bracing idea, which turned out to provide the perfect sound and tone for the later flat-top steel-string guitar.

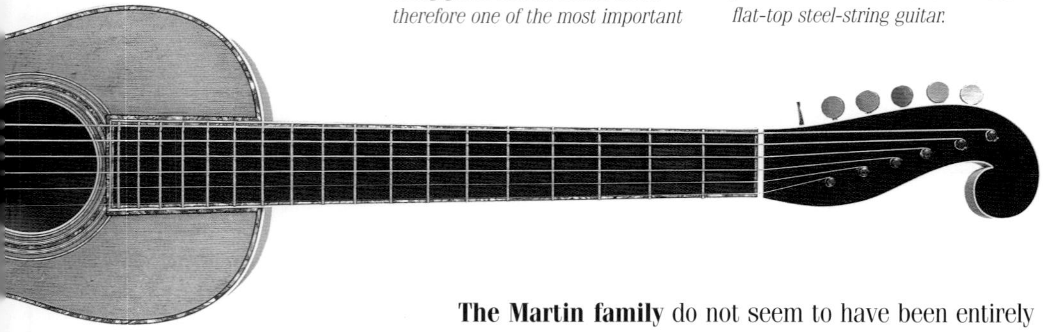

The Martin family do not seem to have been entirely happy in their new home in New York, and a few years after their emigration they were already beginning to plan a move out of the big city. By 1838 Christian Martin had decided on the Lehigh Valley in eastern Pennsylvania as their new home, an area recommended by other German immigrant friends for its similarity to the old country. The Martins moved to Cherry Hill, just outside Nazareth, PA, in 1839.

In the new setting, Martin began to experiment and develop the designs of his guitars, creating a more personal identity and gradually moving away from the styles he had

brought with him to America from Stauffer and Vienna. But as can be seen with a number of the guitars on these pages, Martin wisely did not give up his business dealings with New York after he had moved the 90-plus miles inland to Pennsylvania. It's for similarly good business reasons that Martin instruments continued to be stamped "New York" until the late 1890s – nearly 60 years after the company had moved its workshops away from the city.

John Coupa was a guitarist and guitar teacher who had a teaching studio in New York. He had sold Martin-made instruments to his pupils since the 1830s, and continued to act as a sales outlet for Martin guitars until at least the 1850s, allowing the company to use his Broadway studio as a "showroom." Martin had a much briefer arrangement with

▶ **(Attributed to) STEWART & BAUER**

THIS EXAMPLE: *c1900*

BODY: *14" wide, 3¾" deep*

There are no marks or labels to identify this fine guitar, but a number of experts have suggested that the instrument is most likely the work of Philadelphia makers Samuel S. Stewart and George Bauer.

▼ **WASHBURN STYLE A**

PRODUCED: *c1922-1934 (also as DeLuxe)*

THIS EXAMPLE: *c1928; serial 1835-X/8913*

BODY: *14" wide, 3⅝" deep*

Although usually labeled as the DeLuxe Style 5238 model in contemporary catalogs, this ornate guitar (it has similar decorations to the Bell, below) is stamped "Style A" on the back of the peghead. Some confusion over model names is not

surprising when one considers the uneasy business dealings that were going on behind the Washburn name during the late 1920s and early 1930s, explained in the main text along the bottom of the page. The plaque on the rear of the headstock (shown right) identifies this guitar as being from Washburn's Lyon & Healy era, which ran from the 1880s until around 1928.

out of the guitar business, selling the Washburn name to Tonk, who hired J. R. Stewart, a small Chicago manufacturer, to take over the factory and continue making Washburns.

"In theory the transition was to be smooth," says Newton, "and the only difference would be who actually ran the factory, Stewart instead of Lyon & Healy. It didn't quite work out that way. J. R. Stewart probably went heavily into debt to acquire the Washburn factory, and the onset of the Depression wiped them out. Tonk was left holding the bag, with no one to build Washburns for them.

"They immediately began to look for a successor to Stewart and came up with Regal, another small but presumably more solvent Chicago guitar company." Regal took over the defunct Stewart/Washburn factory and began the production of

Washburns along with a greatly expanded line of Regals. It was the acquisition of the Washburn factory and workers that turned Regal into one of the major manufacturers of the 1930s. For the next dozen years Regal continued to build Washburns for Tonk, although for a short stretch in the late 1930s Gibson apparently took over. By 1939 Regal was back, until production stopped in 1942.

After the war Tonk did not revive the Washburn name, which went unused until the early 1970s when a small company called Beckmen used it on a line of Japanese guitars. Beckmen soon sold the name to a Chicago importer, Fretted Industries Inc., which became Washburn International in 1987 and today merchandises an extensive range of musical instruments, primarily Washburn-brand guitars.

c1894

ORVILLE GIBSON STARTS MAKING INSTRUMENTS

Without Orville Gibson, the carved archtop guitar would not exist. Although the time during which Orville makes his own instruments is relatively brief – from around 1894 to the formation of the Gibson Mandolin-Guitar Co. in 1902 and his departure from that organization in 1903 – it is from these beginnings that the modern archtop guitar will develop and prosper.

◄ O. H. GIBSON GUITAR

PRODUCED: *c1894-1902*

THIS EXAMPLE: *c1898*

BODY: *15¾" wide, 2½" deep*

Orville Gibson invented the idea of the hand-carved archtop guitar, and this is a wonderful example of his ground-breaking craftsmanship. Note the one-piece carved arched top (Orville used mainly spruce) and the similar but flatter back (left; often walnut or maple). The carving meant Orville did not need (or want) internal braces, and he would cut the sides from solid wood. The label inside reads: "The Gibson mandolins and guitars are... recommended by the most expert players in the U.S. as superior to all others," and continues: "Their volume and quality of tone is not equaled by any other instruments... Made by O. H. Gibson, Kalamazoo, Michigan."

▲ O. H. GIBSON MANDOLIN

PRODUCED: *c1894-1902*

THIS EXAMPLE: *c1900*

BODY: *10½" wide, 2½" deep*

Among Orville Gibson's most significant achievements were his mandolin designs. This example, with typical butterfly inlay, is the basis for the revered Gibson F-type. At the time, he devised another notable Gibson mandolin style, the pear-shaped A-type.

◄ MARTIN

THIS EXAMPLE: *c1890s*

BODY: *13¾" wide, 3¼" deep*

This peculiar Martin was apparently custom made by an employee; whatever its origins, it is clearly not in the usual run of Martin models being produced by the factory at the time. Despite apparently dating from the 1890s, the guitar's hourglass shape suggests C. F. Martin's earlier European influences, but the most noticeable construction oddity is the high, or "negative," neckset angle (see side view, left) that tilts the neck slightly forward from its usual position. In fact, this design characteristic was being used 100 years later by American classical guitar maker Thomas Humphrey for his Millennium model. Humphrey described the negative neckset to Acoustic Guitar magazine in 1996: "To me, the harp is the only successful plucked string instrument because its powerful full-bodied sound allows it to hold its own in the orchestra. By sloping the soundboard and using a high neck angle on the Millennium, an entirely different load is created on the soundboard [closer to that of the harp], producing greater power. The elevated fingerboard, which results from the high neck angle, allows incredible access to the upper register," suggests Humphrey.

▲ MARTIN 1-42

PRODUCED: *c1890-1918*

THIS EXAMPLE: *c1895*

BODY: *12⅞" wide, 4⅛" deep*

Martin continued to make elegant flat-top guitars in the late 19th century; the pearl-inlaid Style 42 was introduced in 1870.

▲ C. A. NIGHTINGALE

THIS EXAMPLE: *c1900*

BODY: *12¼" wide, 3⅝" deep*

Other unconventional makers were operating around the same time as Orville Gibson. Charles A. Nightingale worked in Evansville, Indiana, from the mid-1890s. This guitar has his patented secondary internal soundboard, mounted half way down the sides and with a tube connecting to the soundhole, designed to increase volume.

Orville Gibson's early efforts at musical instrument building can be viewed in a number of ways as we look back at them today. Purely as musical instruments, those that have survived the hundred years or more are often hard work to play, even cumbersome. But to hold one of Orville Gibson's guitars or mandolins is to connect with the man whose name was to carry on as one of the greatest and most significant fretted instrument manufacturers of the 20th century – even if Orville's own involvement was brief (see p.25).

Orville Gibson was born on a farm in Chateaugay in upstate New York, close to the Canadian border, in 1856. He first came to Kalamazoo, Michigan, while probably in his early 20s. After working in a shoe store and a restaurant, presumably making instruments and playing in his spare time, he set up as a

manufacturer of musical instruments in Kalamazoo around 1895. It's unclear how Orville learned to make instruments, but he had a refreshingly unconventional mixture of ideas about how to construct the mandolin-family instruments and guitars that he made.

Orville would use carved tops and carved backs, and instead of the usual heated-and-bent sides he would saw the sides from solid wood. All Orville's instrument parts were integrally designed to obviate internal bracing, which he rejects in his 1898 mandolin patent as likely to "rob the instrument of much of its volume of tone and the peculiar excellency thereof." Orville would often have his instrument's bodies decorated with beautiful inlaid pickguards and add a distinctive crescent-and-star to his pegheads.

▼ **MAURER STYLE 590**

PRODUCED: *c1900-1935*

THIS EXAMPLE: *c1930*

BODY: *15" wide, 3⅞" deep*

The Larsons' Maurer brand guitars generally

divided into four different body sizes – Standard, Concert, Grand Concert and Auditorium – as well as three "style" levels of decoration. This beautiful example of Maurer's Style 590 is of the largest body size, Auditorium, and the most ornate style, with magnificent inlay work on peghead, fingerboard and body.

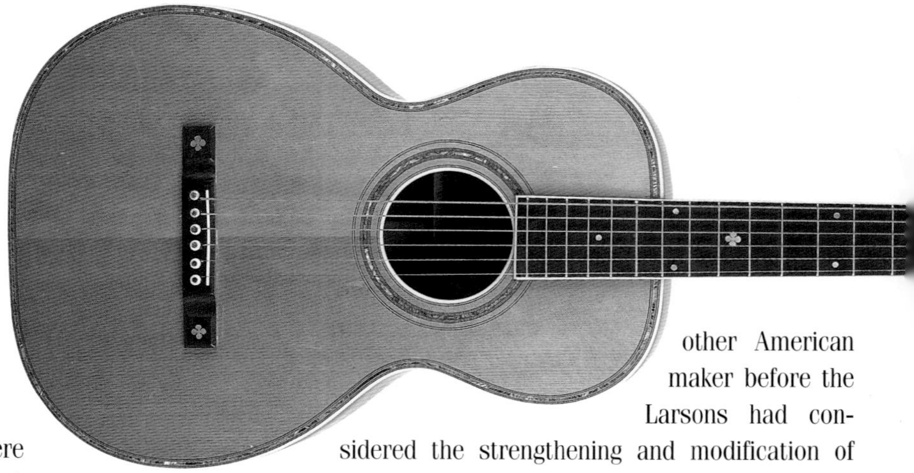

c1900

THE LARSON BROTHERS SET UP IN CHICAGO

Beginning a 40-year run of some superb guitar making, August and Carl Larson take over the Maurer workshop, soon producing Maurer, Stahl and Dyer instruments.

The Larson Brothers were Carl and August Larson, two Swedish immigrants who arrived in Chicago during the 1880s. Their great claim to fame in the story of the American guitar is the fact that their guitars, right from the first examples they made at the very end of the 19th century, were exclusively designed to be fitted with steel strings.

Virtually every other guitar maker at the time was doing what guitar makers had always done – designed instruments for use with gut strings. But the Larsons had noted that mandolins of the period successfully used steel strings to produce a usefully loud sound. While steel strings were certainly available in the late 19th century to fit to guitars, no other American maker before the Larsons had considered the strengthening and modification of construction that a guitar specifically designed for steel strings would require in order to survive.

Consequently, August Larson received a patent in 1904 for the distinctive laminated braces the brothers used for guitar tops: a heavier wood such as rosewood or ebony ("hardwood reinforcements" as they described them) would be stripped between the usual spruce. The Larsons also employed a

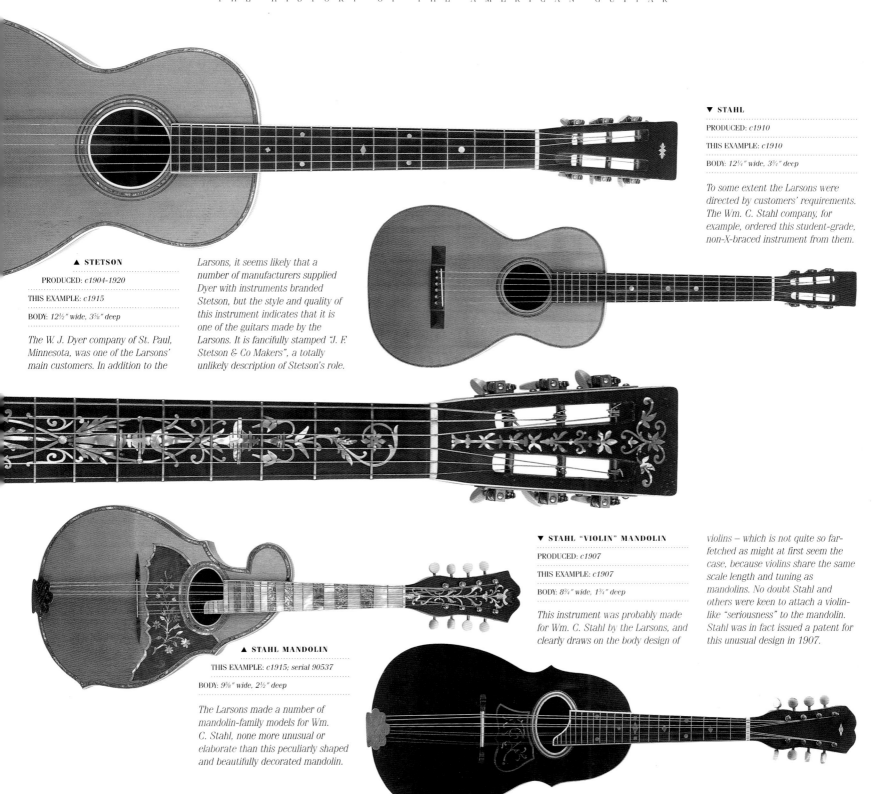

▼ STAHL

PRODUCED: *c1910*

THIS EXAMPLE: *c1910*

BODY: *12¼" wide, 3¾" deep*

To some extent the Larsons were directed by customers' requirements. The Wm. C. Stahl company, for example, ordered this student-grade, non-X-braced instrument from them.

▲ STETSON

PRODUCED: *c1904-1920*

THIS EXAMPLE: *c1915*

BODY: *12½" wide, 3⅝" deep*

The W. J. Dyer company of St. Paul, Minnesota, was one of the Larsons' main customers. In addition to the

Larsons, it seems likely that a number of manufacturers supplied Dyer with instruments branded Stetson, but the style and quality of this instrument indicates that it is one of the guitars made by the Larsons. It is fancifully stamped "J. F. Stetson & Co Makers", a totally unlikely description of Stetson's role.

▼ STAHL "VIOLIN" MANDOLIN

PRODUCED: *c1907*

THIS EXAMPLE: *c1907*

BODY: *8¾" wide, 1¾" deep*

This instrument was probably made for Wm. C. Stahl by the Larsons, and clearly draws on the body design of

violins – which is not quite so far-fetched as might at first seem the case, because violins share the same scale length and tuning as mandolins. No doubt Stahl and others were keen to attach a violin-like "seriousness" to the mandolin. Stahl was in fact issued a patent for this unusual design in 1907.

▲ STAHL MANDOLIN

THIS EXAMPLE: *c1915; serial 90537*

BODY: *9⅜" wide, 2½" deep*

The Larsons made a number of mandolin-family models for Wm. C. Stahl, none more unusual or elaborate than this peculiarly shaped and beautifully decorated mandolin.

▲ STAHL

PRODUCED: *c1904-1935*

THIS EXAMPLE: *c1925*

BODY: *13¼" wide, 3⅝" deep*

Soon after buying Maurer's factory in 1900 the Larsons were making instruments for Stahl, often similar equivalents of Maurer-brand models. This Concert-size example is like a Maurer Style 562½.

noticeable arch to the top and back of their guitars ("built under tension"). A later Larson design had metal rods within the guitar's body to provide even greater internal strength. Given this ingenuity, you might expect the Larsons to be better known. Certainly there are many players and collectors who consider the best of the Larsons' work as among the finest steel-strung flat-top guitars ever made. The Larsons remain obscure because they did not make Larson brand instruments. Instead they manufactured instruments – guitars, harp guitars, mandolins and more – with a variety of brandnames – including Maurer, Stahl, Stetson, Dyer, Prairie State and Euphonon – for a diverse set of outlets.

The Larsons moved into musical instrument making in their newly adopted country during the 1880s, and built their first

instruments probably in the late 1890s under the Champion brand (and possibly some others) for a man called Robert Maurer. He was a music teacher, publisher, instrument manufacturer and distributor, as well as being the owner of at least one retail music store in Chicago.

In 1900 Maurer, whose health was failing, sold his instrument factory to Carl Larson and two other partners who in turn were replaced by August Larson. At first the Larsons continued to use the Maurer brand, and within a few years were also making instruments for W. J. Dyer of St. Paul, Minnesota, and Wm. C. Stahl of Milwaukee, Wisconsin. Both were musical instrument dealers who sold the Larson-made instruments under their own names, with the subtle implication that these were their own products.

▶ **DYER SYMPHONY HARP GUITAR STYLE 8**

PRODUCED: *c1917-1925*

THIS EXAMPLE: *c1920; serial 809*

BODY: *15½" wide, 3⅝" deep*

This particular example of the Larsons' work is an exceptional instrument, much prasied by those lucky enough to have played it. Many musicians and collectors consider the Larsons' quality instruments every bit as good as many of the more revered pre-war Martins.

▲ **KNUTSEN HARP GUITAR**

PRODUCED: *c1898-1917*

THIS EXAMPLE: *c1905*

BODY: *14½" wide, 4¼" deep*

It was Chris Knutsen who at the end of the 19th century came up with this harp guitar design that the Larsons would build upon so successfully.

▲ **DYER SYMPHONY HARP GUITAR STYLE 7**

PRODUCED: *c1917-1925*

THIS EXAMPLE: *c1920; serial 672*

BODY: *15½" wide, 3⅝" deep*

The distinctive long, hollow body extension conjures a uniquely reverberant sound from this surprisingly comfortable guitar, as well as providing an increased bass response that enhances the six sympathetic bass strings.

▲ DYER SYMPHONY HARP MANDOLIN STYLE 25

PRODUCED: *c1912-1925*

THIS EXAMPLE: *c1915; serial 107*

BODY: *9⅛" wide, 2⅝" deep*

Adapting Knutsen's designs to mandolin-family instruments, the Larsons retained the distinctive hollow body-extension to create a sound that a number of Dyer advertisements described as "the full-toned, colorful plectral choir."

◄ DYER SYMPHONY HARP MANDOLIN STYLE 50

PRODUCED: *c1912-1925*

THIS EXAMPLE: *c1918; serial 254*

BODY: *8¾" wide, 2⅝" deep*

Style 50 was the most ornate, decorated variety of the Dyer Symphony harp mandolin line. Other harp-style mandolin-family instruments advertised by Dyer included a mandola and a mandocello. One of the notable aspects of the work of the prolific Larsons is the wide range of instruments that they made, from the smallest to the largest, and in all manner of styles and price ranges.

The Larson Brothers' Dyer Symphony harp guitars are among their finest achievements. These instruments have their roots in the harp guitar design of Chris Knutsen, who received a patent in February 1898 for "a certain new design for a harp-guitar frame."

Little is known about Knutsen. He was living in Port Townsend, Washington, at the time the patent was issued. Knutsen made some harp guitars in his own right, but also produced other instruments for W. J. Dyer, an instrument dealer based in St. Paul, Minnesota.

Knutsen's patent for his harp guitar expired in 1912, and it seems that by about 1917 the Larson Brothers began manufacturing the design for Dyer. They also developed a harp mandolin for Dyer based on the guitar design. The

Larsons had been making instruments for Dyer since around 1904. Knutsen subsequently moved to Los Angeles where he was for a while associated with Hawaiian-guitar maker Hermann Weissenborn (see also p36).

The idea for a harp guitar had originated in Europe at the end of the 18th century, when a classical revival led to a vogue for all things "classical", including hybrids of guitar and lyre (the lyre guitar) and harp and guitar (the harp guitar). Knusten's design is one of the most successful (see also the Gibsons on p26/27 and a variety of harp guitars on p28/29). The Larsons' interpretations for Dyer of Knutsen's design resulted in some astonishingly musical and delightfully responsive instruments that continue to enchant players lucky enough to happen upon one of these rare creations.

▲ LARSON HARP GUITAR

THIS EXAMPLE: *c1920*

BODY: *20" wide, 5" deep*

Although this instrument has no marks or labels to help identify it, it does have some of the characteristic physical and constructional qualities that were commonly used by the Larsons for their instruments. Robert Carl Hartman, grandson of Carl Larson and author of a book on the Larsons, has identified this unusual Gothic-style harp guitar as being the work of the Larsons.

◄ **PRAIRIE STATE "f-HOLE GUITAR"**

PRODUCED: *c1930*

THIS EXAMPLE: *c1930; serial 1523*

BODY: *17½" wide, 4" deep*

The only f-hole model that the Larsons produced came with the Prairie State brand. As Robert Carl Hartman says in his useful book on the Larsons, "Guitars And Mandolins In America," the f-hole Prairie State guitars "ended up somewhere between a flat-top and archtop sound, which thoroughly pleased some people and disgruntled others." The Larsons included their strengthening rod inside, but fitted the instrument with more appropriate "ladder" shaped top bracing, as well as some attractive pearl purfling.

▲ **PRAIRIE STATE "21-INCH SPECIAL"**

PRODUCED: *c1935*

THIS EXAMPLE: *c1935; serial 1113*

BODY: *21" wide, 6⅛" deep*

Some of the Prairie State models made by the Larsons had very large bodies, such as this unprecedentedly enormous example. These guitars were not so heavy as one might expect, however. The Larsons were able to use thinner, lighter woods because of the stability afforded by their strengthening techniques, including the novel rod system (visible above through the soundhole).

▲ **PRAIRIE STATE BASS**

PRODUCED: *c1930s*

THIS EXAMPLE: *c1930s*

BODY: *24" wide, 7" deep*

While some makers had produced mandolin-family basses (see, for example, the Gibson Mando-Bass on p27), the Larsons (as well as others such as Regal) made big basses during the 1930s that had guitar-shaped bodies. These unusual instruments were designed to be played upright like a double-bass, which explains the supporting "spike" fitted to the base of the body.

Prairie State guitars were made by the Larsons from the late 1920s. The most distinctive aspect of the construction of these guitars is the inclusion of a metal strengthening rod within the body, running its length from neck join to base, and visible through the soundhole (see, for example, any of the round-hole examples on these pages).

With typical inconsistency, the Larsons did not use the strengthening rod exclusively for Prairie State branded instruments, but they are the ones most commonly seen with the feature. Also, some instruments have a second, thinner metal rod running almost parallel to the first. This second rod is intended "to restrain the neck from bending forward or coming loose" as a 1930s Larson catalog explained. The Larsons also devised a method for adjusting the neckset angle

by a system of bolts that held the neck to the body. At the time the conventional method of fixing the neck was to glue it in place, as practiced by Martin and Gibson.

August Larson was awarded a number of patents for the rod system, the first of which was issued in June 1930. Like most patents it is written in a strange, convoluted language, but it describes in detail how the rods provide "means for reinforcing guitars and like stringed instruments against the strain of the strings" and "a novel element to counteract the buckling of the instrument from the strain referred to."

The patent goes on to note that the "dowel stick," or strengthening rod, could be made "of reinforced hardwood or of steel tubing," but in production the Larsons in fact opted for the more suitable steel. "In effect," August Larson's 1930

▶ **PRAIRIE STATE**

PRODUCED: *c1927-1944*

THIS EXAMPLE: *c1939*

BODY: *18⅞″ wide, 4″ deep*

Another large-body Prairie State guitar made by the Larson Brothers, this example is very similar in dimensions to the Euphonon model which can be seen on p.22/23. This Prairie State guitar, like a number of examples made by the Larsons, does not have a brandname. However, the instrument is stamped inside the body with two patent numbers, including number 1768261 which is August Larson's first patent, issued in 1930, for the strengthening rod system – a feature usually offered on Prairie State models.

◀ **PRAIRIE STATE STYLE 425**

PRODUCED: *c1927-1944*

THIS EXAMPLE: *c1932; serial 913*

BODY: *14¾″ wide, 3½″ deep*

Like their Maurer brand guitars, the Larsons made Prairie State models in a variety of styles and body sizes, ranging from Style 225 to 450.

▶ **PRAIRIE STATE STYLE 235**

PRODUCED: *c1927-1944*

THIS EXAMPLE: *c1932*

BODY: *13⅜″ wide, 3⅜″ deep*

Style 235 was in Concert size, and a "middle" version of three decorative options. Prairie State prices in the early 1930s ranged from $65 to $100. At the same time Martins ranged from about $25 to $170.

patent concludes, "the dowel stick serves as a firm spacing element for the ends of the instrument body, to prevent them from yielding to the pulling strain of the strings as transmitted by the neck."

All this was designed to make the Prairie State models strong, rigid and durable. And, therefore, to have a commercial advantage. As a catalog from the early 1930s put it: "We have continually improved all our instruments in every way, and a careful inspection and comparison will convince the most critical examiner that they can not be excelled." To some extent the Larsons also exploited the strength of their Prairie State instruments by tending to use lighter, thinner woods in their construction, and this generally resulted in guitars with a quite distinctive, bright sound.

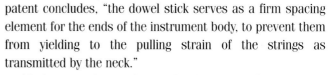

▲ EUPHONON

PRODUCED: *c1935-1944*

THIS EXAMPLE: *c1941; serial 1727*

BODY: *15½″ wide, 4½″ deep*

Euphonon was a brand used by the Larson Brothers to replace Maurer. This example is similar in proportions to the Dreadnought style made by Martin from the early 1930s. Note the fine woods used for the top (above) and the back (below). The Larson instruments do not enjoy the cachet of Martin guitars, but a number of players are beginning to acknowledge how extraordinary they are. If there is a sleeper among instruments in terms of investment potential, maybe it's the Larson guitars.

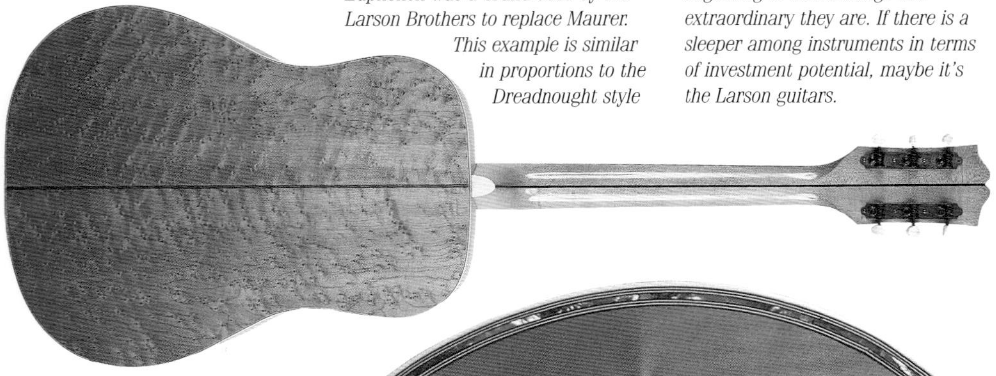

◄ LARSON JAY RICH

THIS EXAMPLE: *Jul. 1939; serial 1552*

BODY: *19" wide, 4" deep*

This magnificent cutaway guitar was specially built by August Larson for country performer Jay Rich. A typed label inside reads: "7-21-39 Custom made for Jay Rich. A. Larson, Chicago. Ser #1552." It's possible this was one of the guitars made by the Larson Brothers for stars of the WLS radio program "National Barn Dance."

► "LARSON GENE COLIN"

THIS EXAMPLE: *c1935*

BODY: *17" wide, 4" deep*

Some of the guitars made by the Larsons for "National Barn Dance" stars had on the peghead a WLS logo or the name of the performer, suggesting this is such an example.

◄ EUPHONON

PRODUCED: *c1935-1944*

THIS EXAMPLE: *c1936; serial 1102*

BODY: *16" wide, 3½" deep*

Unlike this guitar, which is stamped with the customary oval-shape Euphonon brand on the inside of the guitar's back seam, some of the new 14-fret Euphonon-style instruments were sold with Maurer or Prairie State brands through another of the Larsons' Midwest outlets, the Wack Sales Co., which was located in Milwaukee, Wisconsin.

▲ EUPHONON

PRODUCED: *c1935-1944*

THIS EXAMPLE: *c1940*

BODY: *18⅞" wide, 4" deep*

This superb large-body guitar has newspaper photographs of Django Reinhardt stuck inside the body, and it has been suggested that the instrument may at one time have been owned by Reinhardt. Evidence that the Larsons applied different brandnames to broadly similar styles of guitar can be seen by comparing this instrument with the large Prairie State on p.21.

Carl and August Larson managed to devise an appropriate new label for one strand of their musical instrument manufacturing business when they chose Euphonon as a brandname to replace Maurer around 1935. "Euphony" means, quite simply, an agreeable or pleasing sound.

The Larsons had sold instruments using the Maurer brand since buying Robert Maurer's Chicago factory back in 1900, and the Euphonon instruments continued to display some of the hallmarks of the previous Maurer lines – Martin-like proportions abounded, for example.

The Larsons' Euphonon instruments also adopted the contemporary trend toward the more musically convenient and playable arrangement of a 14th fret neck/body join, while they experimented with a variety of larger and generally more unusual design styles. The Larson Brothers also made a small number of guitars for the musicians associated with radio's most popular country music program of the period, *National Barn Dance*, which at its peak attracted an enormous audience of 20 million listeners to Chicago's WLS station.

Carl and August Larson seem to have continued through most of their career effectively as a two-man operation, with Carl the more active in guitar making, and August reportedly running the business and also finding time to take care of guitar finishing. August Larson died in June 1944 at age 71; Carl died two years later at the age of 79. Their guitar manufacturing business died with them, but thankfully the instruments they made will live on for a long time to come.

▲ MARTIN 0-45

PRODUCED: *1904-1939*

THIS EXAMPLE: *1927; serial 33027*

BODY: *13½" wide, 4" deep*

Style 45, Martin's fanciest body yet, came along in the early 1900s. The 0-45 gained an ebony bridge and ivoroid binding from 1918 (ivoroid is a plastic ivory substitute).

▲ MARTIN 00-45

PRODUCED: *1904-1938; 1970-current*

THIS EXAMPLE: *1914; serial 11994*

BODY: *14" wide, 3⅞" deep*

Style 45 was even fancier than Martin's Style 42, extending the pearl inlay and ivory binding further around the body. Martin first displayed Style 45 in its 1904

catalog, saying: "General description same as Style 42... in addition, there is a pearl scroll inlaid in the head and a line of Japan pearl running along the sides on each edge, and on the back." Just in case customers thought this all too ostentatious for Martin's generally reserved and tasteful style, it added: "The pearl is quite narrow and gives a rich effect without being prominent."

1902

C. F. MARTIN INTRODUCES STYLE 45; GIBSON GUITAR-MANDOLIN CO. FORMED

Debuts from Martin's high-end decorative style, and one of the century's most important guitar making companies.

By the turn of the century, changes were in the air at C. F. Martin & Co. Not only was Martin producing guitars, as it had been for over 60 years, but around 1895 the company had entered the mandolin business. Mandolins had been growing in popularity since the 1880s, when they began to jockey for position with banjos and would eventually overtake them as the leading fretted string instruments of the day.

As the 20th century dawned, the guitar was to some extent a poor relation, having difficulty being heard over the din of popular mandolins and banjos. Some guitar builders such as Gibson tried to make their guitars more prominent by constructing them with relatively large body sizes, while others such as the Larson Brothers made guitars that were designed to work with the mandolin's louder steel strings.

Martin reacted to the ideas around it, and introduced a new larger size body option to its line in 1902, the 000. This design had a 15-inch wide body that was nearly an inch wider than the company's previously biggest size, the 00 – which Martin had been offering since 1877.

Elegant simplicity has always been the keynote to Martin design and decoration. The company's earliest guitars, with the exception of some tasteful deployment of ivory and pearl, had generally been plain, straightforward, unencumbered musical instruments. But no doubt the observant industry-watchers at Martin had noticed

▲ GIBSON L-ARTIST

THIS EXAMPLE: c1906; serial 3910

BODY: 13¾″ wide, 2½″ deep

The new Gibson company was formed in 1902, and its earliest guitars generally divided into oval-soundhole models (given an O-series model name) and round soundhole models (with an L-series name). Instruments from the early years sometimes do not exactly match catalog descriptions; the guitar here is an example. "L-Artist" is a name adopted by collectors for instruments with features such as the fancy fingerboard markers seen here that are more extravagant than the examples in period catalogs.

▼ GIBSON STYLE O

PRODUCED: 1902-1923

THIS EXAMPLE: c1905; serial 2622

BODY: 15¾″ wide, 2¾″ deep

Gibson's oval-soundhole Style O guitar carried on from Orville Gibson's innovative tradition of carved archtop instruments. The model went through many changes during its more than 20-year life as Gibson's leading archtop until the introduction of the L-5 in 1922. The guitar shown here is an example of the earliest type of Style O, which can be readily identified by its distinctive "paddle" shape peghead.

▲ GIBSON STYLE O

PRODUCED: 1902-1923

THIS EXAMPLE: c1906; serial 5090

BODY: 18″ wide, 2¾″ deep

Another Style O, but this is from a brief period around 1906 when the model was produced with an extra-large 18-inch wide body. The slotted peghead is a transition from the "paddle" type to Gibson's later more familiar solid design. From about 1908 Style O gained a distinctive "flat" cutaway with a carved scroll.

and remains to this day as the most sought after, desirable Style that Martin produce. Meanwhile, in October 1902, some 600 miles from Martin's HQ in Nazareth, Pennsylvania, a deal was signed by five men in Kalamazoo, Michigan, that formed the Gibson Mandolin-Guitar Manufacturing Company.

Orville Gibson was not one of those five board members, although he was an original shareholder. But by the following summer Orville had sold his shareholding and severed any practical connection with the new Gibson company. For five years Orville received a regular royalty from the board. Then, as Walter Carter writes in *Gibson Guitars: 100 Years of An American Icon*, "In December 1908 [the board] granted him a modest but stable income of $500 a year. They sent him a monthly check of $41.66 until he died in 1918."

how some of Lyon & Healy's Washburn models piled on pearl inlay over bodies and fingerboards. Martin also realized from their new mandolin production that fancier bodies were becoming fashionable. Martin's Style 42 had been introduced in the 1870s with more pearl, and in 1902 Style 45 appeared (initially as a special-order Style 42). First cataloged in 1904, Style 45 is the company's fanciest and most decorated body,

► **GIBSON F-4 CUSTOM MANDOLIN**

THIS EXAMPLE: *c1907; serial 5711*

BODY: *10½" wide, 1½" deep*

The fine fingerboard inlays and extra peghead ornamentation identify this as a custom-ordered model. Its maple neck, not standard at the time, would see fame later with the F-5.

◄ **GIBSON F-2 MANDOLIN**

PRODUCED: *1902-1934*

THIS EXAMPLE: *c1905; serial 2511*

BODY: *10½" wide, 2¼" deep*

Here is an instrument from the early years of the Gibson Mandolin-Guitar Company that retains for the time being many of Orville's hallmarks, including his customary oval soundhole and deep body, a beautifully inlaid pickguard, here with cherubs, and (not shown) a relatively flat, carved back.

◄ **GIBSON STYLE U HARP GUITAR**

PRODUCED: *1902-c1929*

THIS EXAMPLE: *c1906; serial 8544*

BODY: *20¾" wide, 3¾" deep*

Despite the name, this is clearly not designed to be played like a harp. In fact, one plays the normal six-string neck as usual, while the ten sympathetic strings, attached to the peghead extension and "arm," are designed to add sustained bass accompaniment and drones. At first, Gibson's harp guitars were made with 12 sympathetic strings, but by about the time this instrument was built in 1906 the number had been modified to ten. The exceptional fingerboard and peghead inlays were not a standard feature of the Style U harp guitar, and mark out this instrument as another interesting custom order.

The instruments that the fledgling Gibson Mandolin-Guitar Company produced illustrates well how diverse was the range of fretted stringed instruments available in the United States during the early decades of the 20th century. The mandolin was clearly the most popular, and Gibson was setting a path that would lead it to become the most celebrated of mandolin makers, thanks in no small part to its enormously influential F-5 model, introduced in the summer of 1922, a little before the L-5 guitar (see p.30).

But the company's earlier F-type models (like the F-2 and F-4 shown above) set the basic style, based on Orville Gibson's pioneering designs of the late 19th century. The distinctive scrolled body shape was not merely decorative – although of course it helps to lend early Gibson instruments

▶ GIBSON STYLE U HARP GUITAR

PRODUCED: *1902-c1929*

THIS EXAMPLE: *c1912*

BODY: *18¼" wide, 3½" deep*

When compared to the example on the left, this somewhat later example of Gibson's Style U harp guitar shows the changes made to bridge and tailpiece and to the arrangement of the sympathetic strings' tuners. It also has the standard fingerboard markers, and bears the classic slanted "The Gibson" peghead logo which appeared at various times on particular models between the early 1900s and the late 1920s.

▶ GIBSON STYLE J MANDO-BASS

PRODUCED: *1912-c1930*

THIS EXAMPLE: *1920; serial 61434*

BODY: *24¼" wide, 6¼" deep*

Described rather optimistically in a Gibson catalog of the 1920s as "unusually easy to play," the company's Mando-Bass was designed to be played upright like a double-bass – hence the base "spike." But the inclusion of frets on the Mando-Bass's fingerboard encouraged use by players of guitars and mandolin-family instruments, and the Mando-Bass provided the bottom end in the popular and thriving "mandolin orchestras."

such as the mandolins and harp guitars displayed here a commanding physical presence – but also formed one of the interlocking parts of Orville Gibson's design strategy. From his first experiments, Orville began to make the lower part of his necks hollow, providing an extra chamber to assist tonal quality, and gradually adapted this idea into a hollow scroll. Instrument historian Roger Siminoff, who has researched much of the early Gibson story, concludes in *Gibson Guitars: 100 Years Of An American Icon*: "It seems obvious that Orville was fascinated by the addition of this secondary space to the instrument's air chamber."

However, once Orville was out of the Gibson company changes began to be made to his original construction methods, seemingly for reasons of efficiency, ease of

production and, indeed, improvement. Orville's sawed solid-wood sides were replaced with conventional heated-and-bent sides, the hollow chamber in the neck was removed, and the flattish back was made arched, all from about 1907. Also, Orville's inlaid, integral pickguards were replaced around 1908 with a unit elevated from the instrument's surface, devised by Gibson man Lewis Williams (one of the original five Gibson board members of 1902).

Harp guitars were an interesting diversion from standard fretted instrument design around the turn of the century. Gibson became involved along with others such as Chris Knutsen and the Larson Brothers (see p18/19). Gibson also extended its mandolin-family line down to the inevitable lowest-pitched variety, the Mando-Bass, in the early 1910s.

c1910

HARPS, METAL BOARDS AND MUTING BARS

During the first decades of the 20th century a great number of makers, inventors and business people in the United States are feeling their way around the fretted instrument scene, trying to define exactly what kind of instrument the guitar is to become. Here we demonstrate just a few of the schemes and ideas of those years.

◀ **BOHMANN MANDOLIN**

THIS EXAMPLE: *c1910*

BODY: *9¾″ wide, 2¾″ deep*

Joseph Bohmann has been credited by some instrument historians as the first American mandolin maker, beginning in the 1880s. This fine mandolin, although it is without a label or other identifying marks, is constructed in Bohmann's style. Especially distinctive are the extra

strings running inside the body, which may be muted with the switch shown in the detail (above). In fact the difference between the muted and unmuted sound is more musically useful on this mandolin than on the Bohmann harp guitar (main guitar, below left).

◀ **BOHMANN HARP GUITAR**

THIS EXAMPLE: *c1910*

BODY: *20″ wide, 5″ deep*

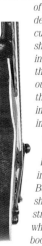

Visually this is a stunning guitar, likened by one observer to some kind of Gothic torture device. The body has a curious "swollen" shape, too (see detail, inset left). With all those strings on the outside of the body and then more still on the inside, it's difficult to imagine what it might sound like. In fact, it turns out to be a beautiful sounding instrument. Like the Bohmann mandolin shown above, it has strings on the inside, while the lever on the body moves the green felt bar inside the soundhole in order to mute the strings. However, because there is a multitude of strings on the outside anyway, there is no discernible difference when you mute those inside. Quite what Bohmann had in mind when they concocted this stranger is anyone's guess, but it seems likely that it was made with a particular customer in mind rather than as a general production item.

▶ **WOLFRAM'S TRIUMPH**

PRODUCED: *c1901-1915*

THIS EXAMPLE: *c1910; serial 5165*

BODY: *16⅛" wide, 4½" deep*

This is one of the stars of this book, demonstrating how a real innovation somehow never caught on. It has a metal fingerboard, which creates a totally different tone for the instrument, sounding somewhere between a regular flat-top and a resonator guitar.

◀ **REGAL HARP GUITAR**

THIS EXAMPLE: *c1930*

BODY: *19" wide, 4⅝" deep*

This unusual Regal-brand harp guitar has all the signs of having been a one-off custom-order model. There do not seem to be any instruments at all similar in any of Regal's published catalogs of the period, although a completely different Regal double-neck harp guitar design had a brief outing in the mid-1930s.

▲ **MAJESTIC HARP GUITAR**

THIS EXAMPLE: *c1920*

BODY: *14½" wide, 4¼" deep*

Gaetano F. Puntolillo was a New York-based inventor who used the Majestic brand for his instruments, primarily banjos which tend to date from the 1920s. This rare harp guitar is based on Chris Knutsen's design, popularized by the Larson-made Dyer instruments (see p.19).

Joseph Bohmann, whose work is seen on the left-hand page, was a German who emigrated from Berlin to Chicago in 1873 at the age of 25. He was issued with a number of American patents for instrument design improvements, and principally made violins, guitars and mandolins, the latter probably among the earliest U.S.-made examples.

With an apparently limitless zeal for publicity, Bohmann (sometimes spelled "Bowman" on patents) rather optimistically advertised himself as "The World's Greatest Musical Instrument Manufacturer," and displayed on some of his labels the medals awarded to him at international instrument competitions, including Atlanta in 1893 and Paris in 1903. He is thought to have died in the 1920s, although some reports have the business in operation as late as 1930.

Not much more is known about Theodore Wolfram, who made the strange metal-fingerboard guitar pictured above. This unusual use of materials would in fact have a second lease on life some 60 years later, when in the mid-1970s the Travis Bean and Kramer companies made electric guitars with aluminum necks – another shortlived venture.

Theodore Wolfram was based in Columbus, Ohio, and had been using the Triumph brandname since the 1890s. Guitar historian Michael Holmes: "In February 1901 Wolfram claimed his 10,000th instrument, but in May the same year announced he was quitting the retail trade to concentrate on manufacture and wholesale. In December the company was declared insolvent and placed in receivership, but Theodore continued in business as the Wolfram Guitar & Mandolin Co."

▼ **GIBSON L-5**

PRODUCED: *1922-1958*

THIS EXAMPLE: *Mar. 1924; serial 76708*

BODY: *16" wide, 3½" deep*

One of Lloyd Loar's exceptional Master Models, the L-5 is where the f-hole archtop guitar began. This example is signed

by Loar. Like other occasional examples within the Master Models, this L-5 is also fitted with a Virzi Tone Producer. This was a wooden disc that was suspended under the guitar's top, inside the body. The Producer was designed to improve tonal qualities, and had some success with violinists rather than players of fretted instruments.

1922

GIBSON LAUNCHES LLOYD LOAR'S MASTER MODELS

Over the following two years the ground-breaking L-5 guitar, F-5 mandolin, H-5 mandola and K-5 mandocello are introduced by Gibson.

Lloyd Loar helped to design Gibson's most distinguished new instruments of the 1920s, the innovative Master Models that included the L-5 guitar and the F-5 mandolin.

At the end of World War I the jazz band replaced the mandolin orchestra as the most popular musical ensemble of the day, and likewise the tenor banjo of jazz replaced the mandolin as *the* popular fretted string instrument. Gibson, whose fortunes before the war had depended largely on the mandolin boom, issued banjos for the first time in the late 1910s. But the significance of a brand new Gibson line of the early 1920s would only really become apparent later.

Introduced between 1922 and 1924, Gibson's Master Models were the L-5 guitar, F-5 mandolin, H-5 mandola and K-5 mandocello. They were like nothing else, featuring violin-style

f-holes rather than round or oval soundholes, and a number of constructional developments and adjustments. The Masters seem significantly different and extensively improved when compared to any of the existing guitars or mandolin-family instruments that Gibson or any other maker produced at the time. But these qualities did not become immediately obvious in an American fretted instrument scene obsessed with the tenor banjo. By the 1930s, however, the L-5 and other f-hole guitars that followed had become the staple of the new breed of jazz guitarists (including the incomparable Eddie Lang). And the F-5 mandolin is now recognized as a great American musical instrument, probably the ultimate mandolin design.

Ted McHugh, who had been an early associate of Orville Gibson in Kalamazoo, worked for the Gibson company from

▲ VIVI TONE ASG

PRODUCED: *c1933-1935*

THIS EXAMPLE: *c1934; serial 240*

BODY: *13¼" wide, 3¾" deep*

Lloyd Loar set up Vivi Tone after his time at Gibson. Loar's idea here was that the back of the guitar (below) was

as important a sounding board as the top. What Loar did was to cut f-holes into the spruce back, and use only a small soundhole under the bridge on the top. As he had with the Master Models, Loar seems to have intended this instrument to work as an integrated whole designed around a sympathetically resonating air chamber.

▼ GIBSON H-5 MANDOLA

PRODUCED: *1923-c1929*

THIS EXAMPLE: *Mar. 1924; serial 76490*

BODY: *11" wide, 2⅛" deep*

In the mandolin orchestra, if the mandolin was equivalent to the violin then the mandola was a viola. This fine H-5 was one of Lloyd Loar's Master Models of the early 1920s. Its printed label inside the body reads: "The top, back, tone-bars and air-chamber of this instrument were tested, tuned and the assembled instrument tried and approved" after which is handwritten in black ink the date (March 31st 1924) and the signature of Lloyd Loar.

1907, and in the early 1920s came up with two important Gibson guitar firsts. One was the adjustable truss rod, designed to reinforce the neck and to be able to correct a neck that has become bent as a result of string tension; the other was the height-adjustable bridge, which makes a playable string-height easier to set. These inventions were both ready in time to be used by Gibson on its Master Models.

Lloyd Loar, an experienced musician, came to work for Gibson in 1919 as a designer (he also fulfilled a number of

▲ EPIPHONE RECORDING D

PRODUCED: *c1927-1932*

THIS EXAMPLE: *c1928; serial 296*

BODY: *15" wide, 3⅝" deep*

Five Recording models – the A, B, C, D and E, most with the innovative sloping cutaway shown here – marked Epiphone's entry to the guitar market in the late 1920s. The peghead design and tuners recall Epiphone's banjo interests, which had begun to fade by this time.

The roots of the Epiphone company go back to the emigration of the Greek Stathopoulo family from Turkey to the United States in 1903. Anastasios Stathopoulo had moved to Izmir (then Smyrna) in Turkey from his native Greece in the 1870s, working as a maker of stringed instruments. When he arrived in New York, Anastasios continued his instrument making business, and when he died in 1915 the business passed to his three sons, Epaminondas ("Epi"), Orphie and Frixo. They made banjos, primarily to meet the growing demand for the jazz-flavored tenor instrument.

Around 1920 Epi seems to have decided that the "House Of Stathopoulo" brand that the brothers were using had become old fashioned, and coined the new Epiphone brandname by appropriately combining his own forename

with the Greek word for "sound" and "voice" (the same word, "phono," had also been adopted quite recently for the phonograph).

In 1924 Epiphone produced the elaborately decorated Recording Series banjos, the success of which led Epi to expand his business by buying the Favoran banjo company in Queens, New York. At the very start of 1928 Epi changed his firm's name to the Epiphone Banjo Company.

It was around this time that Epi launched a line of Epiphone guitars. In retrospect it would seem to have been a very shrewd move, because the U.S. stock market crash of 1929 effectively ended the jazz age, and with it the tenor banjos that had helped fire the music, as well as a good business for banjo makers. While Epi's first guitars were not too successful, they

27

[EPI]PHONE'S "REGORDING
[GUI]TARS" ARE RELEASED

[...] of five curious cutaway-
[...] equipped guitars sees the
Epiphone name appear on
[guit]ars for the first time at the
[en]d of the 1920s. Epiphone is
[n]amed for Epi Stathopoulo, a
[ma]n of Greek extraction who
[em]igrated with his family to the
New York area during the
early 1900s.

▲ **EPIPHONE FT-79**

PRODUCED: *1942-1958*

THIS EXAMPLE: *1944: serial 51913*

BODY: *16" wide, 4¾" deep*

*Epiphone's unusual Recording line of
the 1920s did include some flat-tops,
but this example of the FT-79, a
model that appeared in the early*

*1940s, is typical of the company's
later and relatively more
conventional flat-top models. The
square-shouldered, wide-waisted
shape of the FT-79 is clearly derived
from Martin's dreadnought models
that had debuted in the 1930s.
When Gibson took over Epiphone in
1957, the FT-79 would become the
Texan from the following year.*

SPE
THIS
BODY: 1.

This is as
and only a
Gibson mad
first f-hole g
The original o
ordered the gui
player, Art Prune
can be seen on th
on the peghead.

EPIPH
GUIT

A line

guit
en
na

em

▼ **BELLA VOCE BANJO GUITAR**

PRODUCED: *c1927-1929*

THIS EXAMPLE: *c1928*

BODY: *13¼" wide, 3½" deep*

Gibson entered the banjo market in 1918, but soon competitors such as Bacon and Epiphone were scoring with highly decorated banjos. Gibson hit back with banjos like the elaborately engraved Bella Voce (see back, right). This banjo guitar was a custom order.

▶ **BELLA VOCE BANJO MANDOLIN**

PRODUCED: *c1927-1929*

THIS EXAMPLE: *c1928*

BODY: *13" wide, 3¼" deep*

Here is another highly unusual custom-ordered version of the Bella Voce banjo. This particular instrument grafts a mandolin neck and related string layout on to the body of Gibson's extravagant high-end creation, the Bella Voce banjo.

of musicians but to the laws of physics as well. However, Loar must have decided that he needed independence, and he left Gibson in 1924. Nine years later he formed the Vivi Tone company with ex-Gibson man Lewis Williams, primarily to manufacture electric fretted and violin-family instruments. Electric instruments greatly interested Loar, who had devised an early electric pickup while at Gibson in the 1920s.

Vivi Tone (along with its sister company Acousti-Lectric) made unusual acoustic instruments too – see the example pictured at the top of the opposite page – but Loar and Williams' offerings appear to have been too radical and ahead of their time to make any commercial impact, and within a few years of its inception the company had closed. Lloyd Loar died in the early 1940s, at the age of 57.

nanagerial roles) and would later be described as Gibson's Acoustic Engineer." It was Loar's technical improvements to he Master Models, especially the custom "tuning" he mployed to ensure that each instrument performed at a olistic peak, that make them so valued today. Loar would ndividually carve and adjust each top, back, internal tone ars and f-holes, "tuning" the entire evolving instrument as e went, in order to achieve as near perfect a sonic package s he could, and one that was attuned not only to the needs

▼ EPIPHONE RECORDING E

PRODUCED: *c1927-1932*

THIS EXAMPLE: *c1929; serial 382*

BODY: *15⅜" wide, 3¾" deep*

Not noted in surviving documents of the period, this rare example of the top-of-the-line Recording model is without the cutaway of the guitars shown in contemporary catalogs.

▲ KEY-KORD UKULELE

PRODUCED: *c1929-1931*

THIS EXAMPLE: *c1930*

BODY: *11⅛" wide, 3⅛" deep*

This odd instrument snows that Epiphone was not alone in hinting at the possibilities of a cutaway. Key-Kords were made by the Chicago Stromberg-Voisinet company (changed to the more familiar Kay in 1931). Devised to let people play the fashionable ukulele without actually learning to play, the fingerboard-mounted device has 21 different chord buttons. Each is linked to a mechanism underneath that forms chords on the fingerboard.

▲ EPIPHONE MADRID

PRODUCED: *c1936-1942 (this style)*

THIS EXAMPLE: *1936; serial 10331*

BODY: *16" wide, 4¾" deep*

In its earliest manifestation the Madrid had been among Epiphone's earliest full-bodied flat-top guitars. It *was offered primarily as a Hawaiian guitar and unusually, like Gibson's HG-24 (see p.37), came with no less than four f-holes. However, around 1936 the model was revamped to the style shown here, complete with a conventional round soundhole as well as the large, full body size that was becoming fashionable at the time.*

Probably as a competitive hint at Gibson's "Master Models," Epiphone used the odd "Masterbilt" name for its high-end instruments throughout the 1930s, as well as for various accessories such as strings (above).

identified the Epiphone name as a guitar brand and marked Epi as one of the few established banjo makers who was clever enough to switch from the outmoded banjo to the instrument of the future – the guitar.

That first Epiphone guitar line bore the same Recording name as the company's earlier banjos. No doubt someone with Epi's business acumen would have been pleased by the association that the similarity of the names of his new Epiphone Recording guitars implied with the ever-more-popular phonograph and its reproduction of recorded music.

There are five known Recording models, publicized as "The New Epiphone Recording Guitars" in a 1928 catalog. Each of the Recording models shown in that brochure stands out instantly thanks to an unusual sloping cutaway to the body (as

seen on the guitar pictured on the left). While it is not the type of cutaway with which we are familiar today, Epiphone's early take on the cutaway idea does at least acknowledge the player's point of view. The more modern cutaway shape would become established following Gibson's popularization of the concept from the late 1930s. But it was only when electric guitars began to grab players' imaginations that a more convincing musical argument for the wider adoption of the cutaway would be made.

Epiphone's Recording guitars did not last long, and by the early 1930s the company would come out with a new line of archtop models, the Masterbilt series. These would provoke reaction from a dormant Gibson and provide the basis for Epiphone's more modern archtops (see p.68).

1927

THE HAWAIIAN INFLUENCE CONTINUES

Hawaiian music had first become an enormously popular fad in America back in the 1910s. But as we discover on these pages, the Hawaiian style was still having an important and strong effect on guitar sales and guitar marketing well into the 1920s and the 1930s.

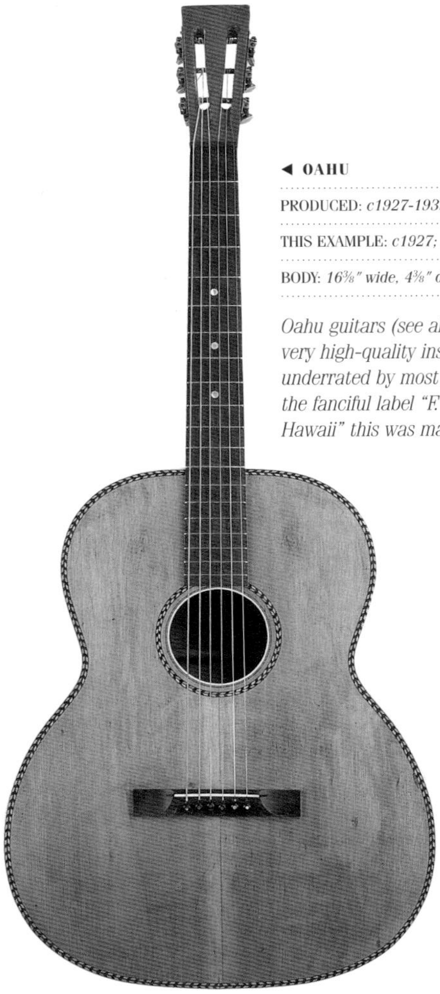

◄ OAHU

PRODUCED: *c1927-1935*

THIS EXAMPLE: *c1927; serial 20081*

BODY: *16⅜" wide, 4⅛" deep*

Oahu guitars (see also below) are very high-quality instruments, underrated by most players. Despite the fanciful label "F. W. Konkua, Hilo, Hawaii" this was made by Kay.

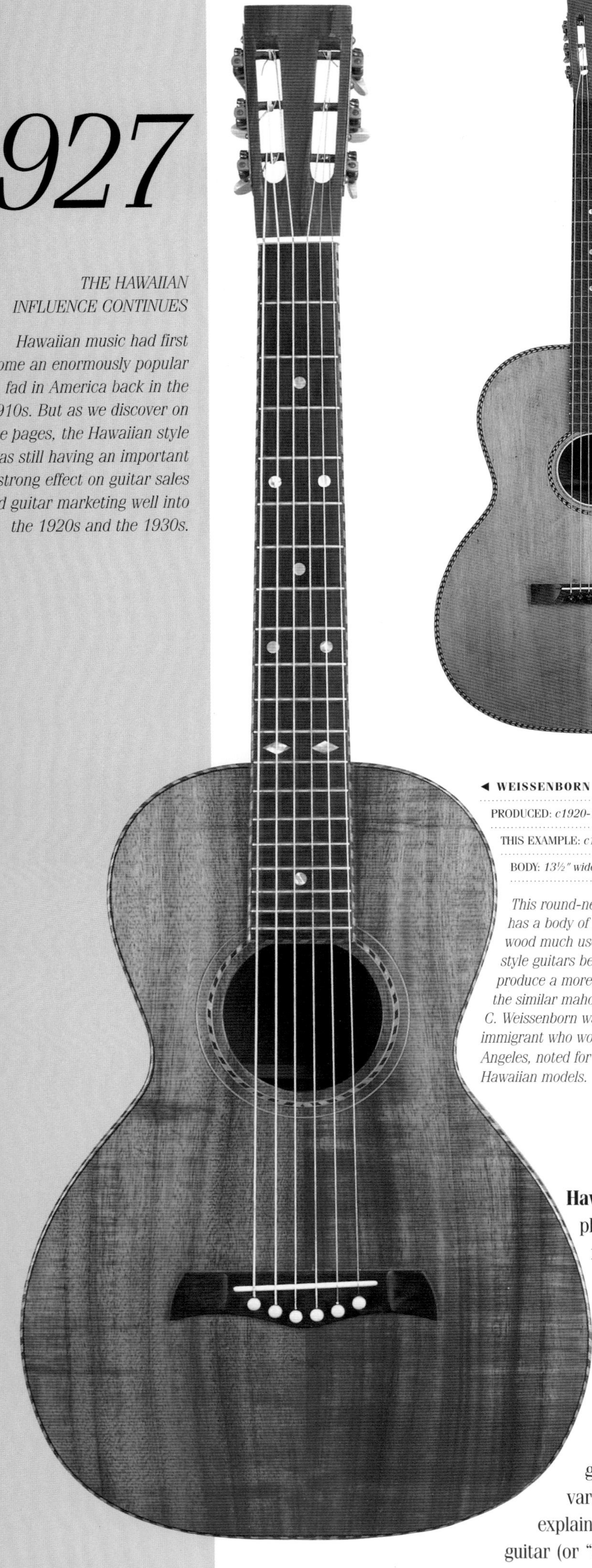

◄ WEISSENBORN STYLE C

PRODUCED: *c1920-1930*

THIS EXAMPLE: *c1925; serial B-3-S1*

BODY: *13½" wide, 4¼" deep*

This round-neck Spanish guitar has a body of koa, a Hawaiian wood much used for Hawaiian-style guitars because it is said to produce a more suitable tone than the similar mahogany. Hermann C. Weissenborn was a German immigrant who worked in Los Angeles, noted for his hollow-neck Hawaiian models.

Hawaiian music is usually considered by guitar players as the source for two important developments. First (and without forgetting African roots) for popularizing slide guitar playing in the U.S. in the early years of the 20th century; and second, for the Hawaiian guitar itself. Some time in the 19th century players in Hawaii had hit upon a nostalgic, drifting sound by sliding a metal object – maybe a comb or a knife or a piece of tubing – across a guitar's strings, which they customarily set to various open-chord or "slack key" tunings. All this explains why slide guitar is sometimes called Hawaiian guitar (or "steel guitar" for the steel object used to press

▲ OAHU DELUXE JUMBO 68

PRODUCED: *c1933-1939*

THIS EXAMPLE: *c1936*

BODY: *15½" wide, 3⅞" deep*

Oahu was a great marketing scheme started in 1927 by Harry Stanley to sell Hawaiian guitar-playing courses. Despite offices in Cleveland, Ohio, Stanley advertised "Honolulu Conservatories" and "studios in all large cities." He had a line of Oahu guitars made, too, like this Kay-built square-neck.

► **OSCAR SCHMIDT 'KOA'**

THIS EXAMPLE: *c1920s*

BODY: *14⅝" wide, 3⅞" deep*

The Oscar Schmidt company ran out of Jersey City, New Jersey, and offered a number of different guitar brands. This example may have been one of their upscale Sovereign line, given the nicely decorated fingerboard and pickguard. The koa body would tend to place the guitar in the Hawaiian-crazy period during the 1920s.

◄ **GIBSON HG-24**

PRODUCED: *c1929-1932*

THIS EXAMPLE: *1929; serial 88697*

BODY: *16" wide, 4½" deep*

This shortlived model is of great historical importance because it is the first guitar with a 16-inch-wide body of dreadnought proportions with the neck joining the body at the 14th fret. Of much interest but less importance are its extra "internal" body wall and the four f-holes. Despite the HG model name (for Hawaiian Guitar) this and the few other surviving examples are set up for normal "Spanish" play.

◄ **MARSHALL SPECIAL**

THIS EXAMPLE: *c1930*

BODY: *15" wide, 4" deep*

This is identical to a model made by Gibson that is more often seen with a Kel Kroyden brand. It is typical of the large numbers of instruments with Hawaiian-flavored scenes that were sold in the wake of the Hawaiian music craze which lasted from the 1910s into the 1930s. Kel Kroyden and Marshall were probably retailers who bought own-brand guitars from Gibson.

against the strings). The main requirements of the Hawaiian guitar itself are a raised nut to shift the strings well clear of the fingerboard (often adapted with non-existent or special low frets), so that the player can slide away without fear of noisy collisions, and a straight, non-compensated bridge saddle, so that the slide can be held perpendicular to the strings. Also, some Hawaiian guitars have a neck that is "square" in cross-section rather than the usual rounded type.

Hawaiian musicians had already had commercial successes in the United States by the end of the 19th century, but it was the raging success of the Hawaiian pavilion at the San Francisco Panama-Pacific-International Exposition of 1915 that really kicked the Hawaiian music craze into top gear in America. The official history of the Exposition

reported: "People were about ready for a new fad in popular music at the time of the Exposition and the sweet voices of the Hawaiians... were enough to start a musical vogue."

Hit records followed, including 'Along The Way To Waikiki' by Frank Ferera, who had been one of the guest guitarists at the Exposition. Americans bought armfuls of Hawaiian records, and then bought Hawaiian guitars so that they could play the music too. Guitar makers responded enthusiastically to this enormous demand, and the Martin company was one of the first to make guitars especially for Hawaiian playing, introducing its 0-28K model in 1917. At a time when jazz and its tenor banjo were growing in popularity, the Hawaiian craze provided a solid market for guitar makers, and underlined a new-found appeal and widespread approval for the guitar.

1927

NATIONAL INTRODUCES FIRST RESONATOR GUITARS

John Dopyera and George Beauchamp come up with one of the great mechanical marvels of the 1920s, and Dopyera's company National brings out the shiny, loud "ampliphonic resonator" guitars at the end of the decade. They are based on a clever internal mechanical system using three aluminum cones to capture, amplify and project the guitar's sound.

◄ **NATIONAL STYLE 2 TENOR**

PRODUCED: *c1927-1930*

THIS EXAMPLE: *c1928; serial 221*

BODY: *14⅛" wide, 3" deep*

Nationals of this period were made in one of four major Styles: 1, 2, 3 and 4. As well as six-string guitars in Spanish and Hawaiian set-ups, National also made tricone resonator-type ukuleles, mandolins, tenor guitars (21 frets, 23-inch scale) and plectrum guitars (22 frets, long neck with 27-inch scale). Tenor guitars, such as this National Style 2 example, were introduced during the 1920s sporting four strings (tuned C-D-G-A) on a narrow neck to encourage banjo players to move to the guitar, which was gaining in popularity.

◄ **NATIONAL STYLE 4 'TRICONE'**

PRODUCED: *c1927-1938*

THIS EXAMPLE: *c1931; serial FS-2626*

BODY: *14¼" wide, 3⅛" deep*

The three-cone ("tricone") ampliphonic resonator system invented by National can be seen as three discs through the soundholes on the body (left). Underneath the T-section cover is a T-shaped bridge which passes the strings' vibration to the three spun-aluminum cones. The

three cones resonate and move in and out like loudspeakers, amplifying the sound and providing the instrument with a loud, brash tone that is short on sustain but has a character and timbre all its own. This sublime art deco guitar is a Style 4 with a Hawaiian-style square neck. Style 4 was National's top model of the time, identifiable by the fancy pearloid overlay on the headstock, as well as its highly engraved body (best seen on the back, which is shown above, center).

◄ **NATIONAL STYLE 2 'TRICONE'**

PRODUCED: *c1927-1938*

THIS EXAMPLE: *1928; serial 0400*

BODY: *14¼" wide, 3⅛" deep*

National's metal bodies were made from nickel-plated "German silver," a silver colored alloy comprised of a mixture of nickel, copper and zinc.

► **NATIONAL 'TRICONE'**

PRODUCED: *c1936*

THIS EXAMPLE: *c1936; serial A3709*

BODY: *14¼" wide, 3¼" deep*

This unusual National does not appear in any of the company's catalogs. It's possible that it may be an early or trial version of the Style 97 that National brought out in 1936.

▲ **NATIONAL STYLE 1 UKULELE**

PRODUCED: *c1928-1935*

THIS EXAMPLE: *c1932; serial 305*

BODY: *7" wide, 2" deep*

Another result of the Hawaiian music boom of the 1910s and 1920s (see p.36) was the rise of the ukulele (a word that means "leaping flea" in Hawaiian), an instrument derived from the machête da braça brought to Hawaii by immigrants from Madeira at the end of the 19th century. National like many guitar makers found the ukulele business useful to sustain them through the tenor banjo era.

"**More volume!**" cried the guitarist of the 1920s and 1930s. Guitar makers responded in various ways: some produced instruments with larger bodies, others tried to amplify the guitar by fixing pickups to the body. In California, the stylish "ampliphonic resonator" guitar, an effective reaction to the volume problem, was launched by the National company. The resonator guitar used the novel idea of suspending resonating aluminum cones that act something like loudspeakers inside a metal body, making for a loud, distinctive instrument.

Depending on which of the various stories one believes, the resonator principle was invented either by John Dopyera or by George Beauchamp – more likely, a combination of the two. John Dopyera was one of three brothers (also Rudy and Ed) who, after emigrating from Czechoslovakia, set up National in California in the mid-1920s, at first to produce the metal tenor banjo that John had invented. George Beauchamp was a vaudeville guitarist and keen tinkerer who was one of the performers of the time calling for louder guitars. Beauchamp apparently first approached Dopyera with a request to fit a peculiar horn attachment to a guitar in order to increase its volume. From that transaction followed the rather more practical resonator scheme, and Beauchamp joined National.

National's first "tricone" resonator guitars came out in 1927. A complicated set of business maneuvers followed. The Dopyera brothers split from National after an argument and formed Dobro during 1929 to make single-cone resonator guitars (p.42). Dobro then licensed production to Regal (p.46), and Dobro and National were merged again in 1935.

▼ **GIBSON A-C CENTURY MANDOLIN**

PRODUCED: *c1934-1937*

THIS EXAMPLE: *1935*

BODY: *10" wide, 1⅞" deep*

*Gibson's A-style pear-shaped
mandolin design dates*

*back in essence to Orville Gibson,
but has seen many varieties and
reinterpretations. Few were as
striking as this Century model of the
1930s, one of the instruments that
Gibson named for the 1933/34
Century Of Progress Exposition at
the Chicago World's Fair.*

1928

*GIBSON'S FIRST
"SIGNATURE" GUITAR*

*Nick Lucas croons hits, and
teases the frets on early guitar
solo records. Gibson cannot
resist, and issues the
Nick Lucas Model.*

The "signature" guitar, where a famous musician endorses a particular instrument named for him or her, is a familiar sight today. Back in the 1920s, when Gibson brought out their Nick Lucas model, it was a new idea in American guitars.

Nick Lucas (born Dominic Nicholas Anthony Lucanese in Newark, New Jersey, in 1897) was the first American to became a big star as a result of making popular guitar-and-vocal records. In the 1920s Lucas, touted as "the Crooning Troubadour," made big hits like 'Tiptoe Through The Tulips' and 'I'm Looking Over A Four-leafed Clover,' as well as recording some early guitar-orientated solo tracks such as 'Pickin' The Guitar' and 'Teasin' The Frets.'

Lucas eventually sold over 80 million records, and such fame, along with his guitar method books, did much to popularize the guitar at a time when the banjo and various Hawaiian-inspired instruments were generally more in evidence in America. Gibson pounced onto this famous guitarist as someone who could help sell its guitars to a wider audience, and in 1928 the company launched the Nick Lucas Model (sometimes called the Nick Lucas Special in catalogs) that would last in the line for ten years. Lucas in fact continued to play the Gibson L-1 flat-top that he'd always used – he could even be seen clutching the L-1 in the picture of him on the Gibson label inside the Nick Lucas Model.

Gibson's catalog of 1928 contained some stirring prose on the subject of its new $125 model: "The wizardry of Nick Lucas and his guitar is known to all music lovers. Combining his ideas and knowledge with the skill of Gibson Artist-

▼ GIBSON NICK LUCAS "FLORENTINE"

THIS EXAMPLE: c1928; serial 85102

BODY: 13¾" wide, 4½" deep

Gibson issued the regular Nick Lucas Model in 1928, named for 1920s crooning guitar star Nick Lucas. But this custom-ordered Nick Lucas instrument has a spectacularly inlaid

fingerboard, based on the design that was used for the fingerboard of Gibson's Florentine banjo, another over-the-top display of Gibson art that had appeared in 1927. It's interesting that Gibson did the kind of things that Martin, for example, would never have done, and as a result Gibson produced some very adventurous decoration. It's also

interesting to speculate what Nick Lucas himself would have made of this wonderful instrument. Lucas did a great deal to popularize the sound of the steel-string flat-top guitar with his chart successes in the 1930s. The regular Gibson Nick Lucas model stayed in the company's line until 1938. A modified reissue appeared in 1991.

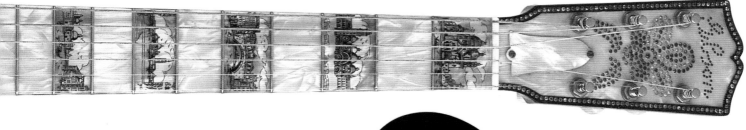

▼ GIBSON L-75

PRODUCED: 1932-c1933 (this style)

THIS EXAMPLE: c1932

BODY: 14½" wide, 3⅜" deep

This rare guitar completes the fabulous trio of Gibson's "Century" instruments, and in a sense these

three items sum up an era of hope and excitement. The Gibson company issued very few L-75s with this ornate Century style of fingerboard, and by 1934 the L-75 had been changed to a much more ordinary instrument that came merely with dot fingerboard inlays and a standard Gibson peghead.

▲ GIBSON L-C CENTURY

PRODUCED: 1933-1939

THIS EXAMPLE: c1934

BODY: 14½" wide, 4¼" deep

The L-C was the flat-top representative of the Century

models, and was effectively part of Gibson's line of L-style flat-tops during the 1930s (the other two were the L-1 and L-00). These guitars and others like them manage to prove just how much sound and character can be had from a small-bodied flat-top instrument.

craftsmen has given birth to a truly magnificent guitar. Here is an instrument with big, harp-like tone, responsive to the lightest touch, balanced in every register. Crisp, sparkling treble and solid resonant bass that makes your whole being sway to its rhythmic pulsations. To play it is to know a measure of the same inspiration that has carried Nick Lucas to great heights. You love the feel as it comes to life with the touch of your fingers. Your regard grows like a rare flower watered by the crystal drops of purest melody. It is indeed an instrument by an artist, for an artist." In fact, it was quite a good guitar. The example shown above in the main picture is a special custom-

ordered version with a non-standard highly decorated fingerboard and peghead; the regular Nick Lucas Model had less ornate inlays on a bound rosewood fingerboard, as well as the model's distinctively small but unusually deep body.

Meanwhile, Gibson went pearloid crazy in the 1930s, offering a set of decorated instruments that used the plastic pearl substitute for an onslaught of fancy fingerboards and pegheads. Two of the models – the L-C Century guitar and the A-C Century mandolin – were named for the 1933/1934 Century Of Progress Exposition at the Chicago World's Fair, which Gibson clearly had not failed to notice taking place just the other side of Lake Michigan. Another guitar, the rare early type of the L-75 model, matched the Century models for pearloid encrustation and pearl-and-rosewood inlays.

1929

THE DOPYERA BROTHERS BEGIN DOBRO PRODUCTION

Splitting off from the National company he co-founded, John Dopyera begins to make a new line of redesigned wood-body (and later metal-body) resonator guitars in California. The new guitars have the Dobro brandname. A parallel line licensed to and made by Regal appears in the 1930s, and Dobro itself moves to Chicago in 1936.

◄ DOBRO MODEL 55

PRODUCED: *1929-1933 (also as Model 56)*

THIS EXAMPLE: *c1930*

BODY: *14" wide, 3" deep*

The Dopyera brothers were Czech immigrants who had settled in L.A. in the early years of the 20th century. This Model 55 is the first style of guitar that their Dobro company began to make in its Los Angeles factory in 1929, after the Dopyeras had left National to set up on their own.

◄ DOBRO NO. 100

PRODUCED: *c1930-1937 (also as No. 108)*

THIS EXAMPLE: *c1935; serial 7500*

BODY: *14" wide, 3" deep*

The new Dobro resonator guitars had a revised single cone of a different shape in place of National's three. Also, instead of the T-shape bridge of the Nationals, Dobro guitars had a bridge which connected to the cone by an eight-legged "spider" (partly visible here through the body-plate holes). Another obvious difference is that the early Dobros have wooden bodies, as opposed to the metal Nationals. John Dopyera said this was because they could not afford at first to tool up to make expensive metal bodies. For all these reasons, Dobros tend to sound quite different than Nationals, and are less acceptable to some players.

National's tricone "ampliphonic resonator" instruments, first marketed in 1927, had three aluminum cones fitted inside the guitar's body (see p.38). The cones acted effectively like loudspeakers, amplifying the sound of the strings and providing a loud instrument with a distinctive tone.

Arguments developed at National in California early in 1929 about the design of a proposed single-cone resonator instrument, and John Dopyera and his two brothers, Ed and Rudy, left the company in disgust. The three ex-National men formed the Dobro Manufacturing Company (the Dobro name came from an amalgamation of the first letters

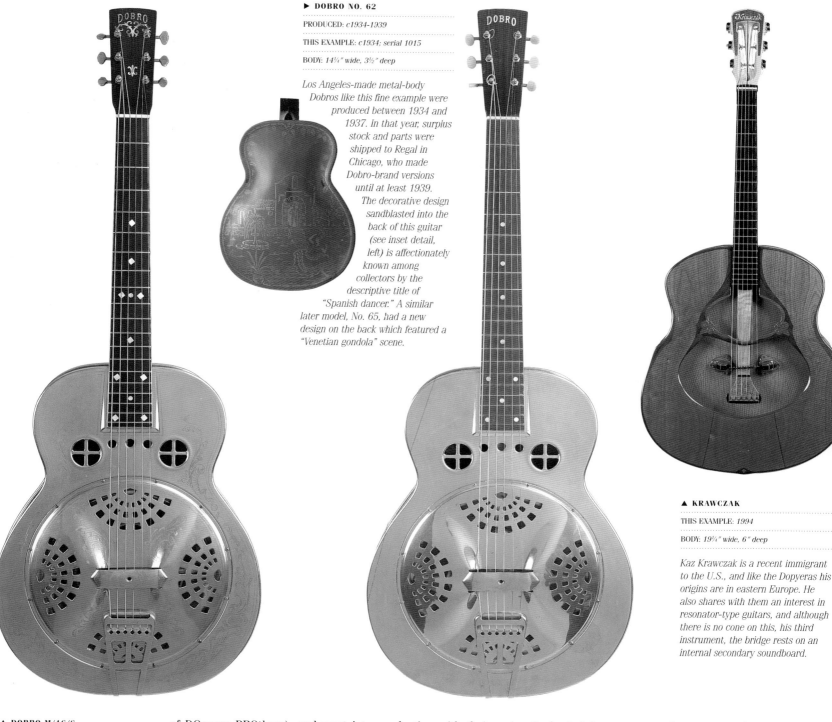

► DOBRO NO. 62

PRODUCED: *c1934-1939*

THIS EXAMPLE: *c1934; serial 1015*

BODY: *14¼" wide, 3½" deep*

*Los Angeles-made metal-body
Dobros like this fine example were
produced between 1934 and
1937. In that year, surplus
stock and parts were
shipped to Regal in
Chicago, who made
Dobro-brand versions
until at least 1939.
The decorative design
sandblasted into the
back of this guitar
(see inset detail,
left) is affectionately
known among
collectors by the
descriptive title of
"Spanish dancer." A similar
later model, No. 65, had a new
design on the back which featured a
"Venetian gondola" scene.*

▲ KRAWCZAK

THIS EXAMPLE: *1994*

BODY: *19¼" wide, 6" deep*

*Kaz Krawczak is a recent immigrant
to the U.S., and like the Dopyeras his
origins are in eastern Europe. He
also shares with them an interest in
resonator-type guitars, and although
there is no cone on this, his third
instrument, the bridge rests on an
internal secondary soundboard.*

▲ DOBRO M/16/S

PRODUCED: *c1934-1937*

THIS EXAMPLE: *c1934; serial 1085*

BODY: *14⅛" wide, 3½" deep*

*Dobro began to make metal-body
guitars in Los Angeles in 1934, while
the licensed Regal versions made in
Chicago appeared the following year
(see p.46). The M/16 was Dobro's
top Los Angeles-made metal guitar,
with a nickel-alloy body and
especially elaborate engraving.*

of DOpyera BROthers), and went into production with their wooden-body version of the single-cone resonator instrument. Guitar historian Mike Newton: "As soon as the Dobro hit the market they found themselves in a ferocious legal battle with George Beauchamp at National who was scaring off potential Dobro dealers by claiming Dobros infringed on National patents. This state of war went on for a couple of years, with Dobro suing National for $2 million at one point. In the meantime, two other Dopyera brothers, Louis and Robert, were brought in as investors in 1930, and the company was reorganized as Dobro Corporation Ltd."

Things calmed down when Louis Dopyera bought a chunk of National stock and Beauchamp was fired by National (partly for helping to set up the company that would make Rickenbacker guitars – see p.68). Around the start of 1933 Dobro licensed Regal to manufacture Regal-brand Dobros, and the resulting increase in production gave National some real competition. A merger in 1935 led to National-Dobro Inc. and a new single factory, although the production lines and marketing of the brands were kept separate. The new operation moved to Chicago in early 1936. Mike Newton: "Regal was given exclusive rights to manufacture Dobros in '37, although a few were still finished up at the L.A. factory. Dobro then begins to fade in importance." Ed and Rudy Dopyera recovered the Dobro name in 1971, and their company, O.M.I., was bought by Gibson in the 1990s.

▲ **MARTIN OM-45 CUSTOM**

THIS EXAMPLE: *1983; serial 445107*

BODY: *15⅛" wide, 3⅞" deep*

While there are many fans of old Martins, there are probably just as many players who love their new guitars. For example, Martin started making the OM-45 again in 1977; this very special custom example has some exceptional extra inlay on both the fingerboard and the pickguard.

▲ **MARTIN OM-45**

PRODUCED: *1930-1932, 1977-current*

THIS EXAMPLE: *1930; serial 44553*

BODY: *14⅞" wide, 3¼" deep*

It is said that this beautiful guitar was purchased by the White House from a Washington DC music store so that at a White House ceremony in the early 1930s President Hoover could present it to a man prominent in the local broadcasting industry. While this story does add great interest to this instrument, the OM is anyway one of the finest flat-top guitars of all time, and this example is especially fine. Martin's "Orchestra Model" combines wonderfully the sheer volume of a dreadnought guitar with the tonal balance of a smaller-body instrument, and as a result produces what is a quite extraordinary fingerstyle guitar.

1929

MARTIN MAKES ITS FIRST "14-FRET" GUITAR

After a request from banjo player Perry Bechtel, Martin introduces the "long-neck" Orchestra Model (OM), easing the path of banjoists to the newly popular guitar.

▲ **MARTIN 2-44 OLCOTT-BICKFORD ARTIST**

PRODUCED: *1930*

THIS EXAMPLE: *1930; serial 43719*

BODY: *12⅛" wide, 3⅞" deep*

Classical guitarist and teacher Vahdah Olcott-Bickford ordered a series of special high quality student guitars from Martin between the early 1910s and the late 1930s. She wanted the excellence of Style 45, but without the overt pearl trim. The special result was called Style 44, and only a little over 30 were made, the majority in size 0. This 2-44 Olcott-Bickford model is one of just four that Martin produced, and was Olcott-Bickford's personal guitar.

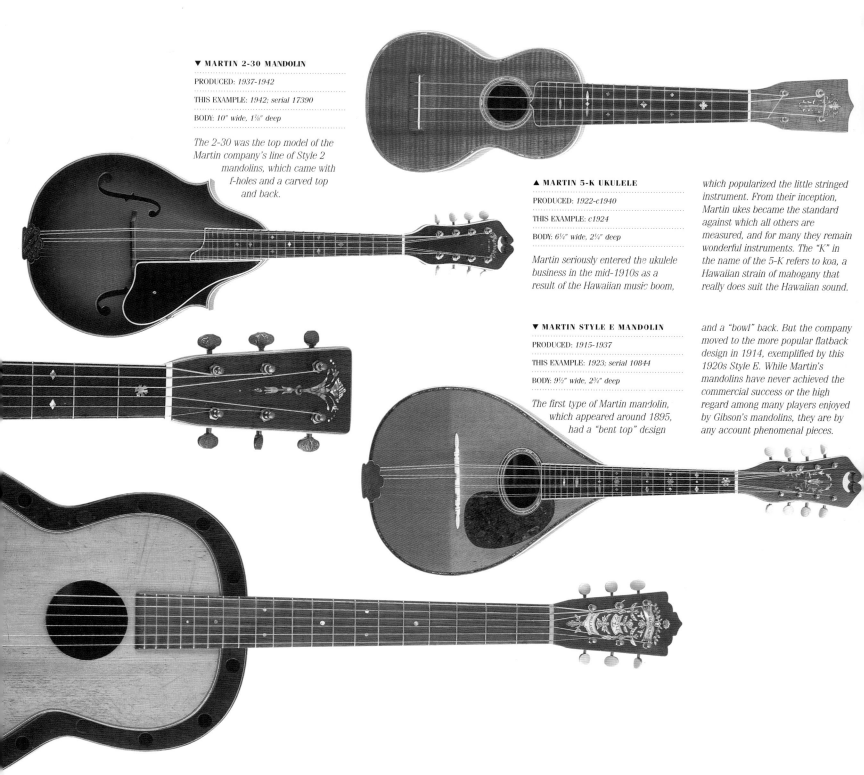

▼ MARTIN 2-30 MANDOLIN

PRODUCED: *1937-1942*

THIS EXAMPLE: *1942; serial 17390*

BODY: *10" wide, 1⅞" deep*

The 2-30 was the top model of the Martin company's line of Style 2 mandolins, which came with f-holes and a carved top and back.

▲ MARTIN 5-K UKULELE

PRODUCED: *1922-c1940*

THIS EXAMPLE: *c1924*

BODY: *6¼" wide, 2¼" deep*

Martin seriously entered the ukulele business in the mid-1910s as a result of the Hawaiian music boom,

which popularized the little stringed instrument. From their inception, Martin ukes became the standard against which all others are measured, and for many they remain wonderful instruments. The "K" in the name of the 5-K refers to koa, a Hawaiian strain of mahogany that really does suit the Hawaiian sound.

▼ MARTIN STYLE E MANDOLIN

PRODUCED: *1915-1937*

THIS EXAMPLE: *1923; serial 10844*

BODY: *9½" wide, 2¼" deep*

The first type of Martin mandolin, which appeared around 1895, had a "bent top" design

and a "bowl" back. But the company moved to the more popular flatback design in 1914, exemplified by this 1920s Style E. While Martin's mandolins have never achieved the commercial success or the high regard among many players enjoyed by Gibson's mandolins, they are by any account phenomenal pieces.

▲ PARAMOUNT STYLE L

PRODUCED: *c1930*

THIS EXAMPLE: *c1930; serial 101*

BODY: *13⅜" wide, 4" deep*

This rare Martin-made guitar with its unusual "double" body is one of many attempts that were being made at the time to achieve more

volume. Best known for banjos, the Paramount brand was sold by Wm. L. Lange to the Gretsch company during the early 1940s.

During the 1920s the guitar began to increase in popularity, and some players began to question the designs offered to them by the major makers. Perry Bechtel was a multi-instrumentalist whose work on banjo in particular meant that he was used to having the whole fingerboard available for melodic flights. But when, like many banjo players who needed to move with the times, he turned to the newly popular guitar, he would often stumble on a wide neck that joined the body at the 12th fret, finding it hard work to play any higher. So Bechtel went to Martin and made a simple request: "Can you make me a guitar that feels like a banjo?"

Martin complied, building in 1929 a special 000-28 for Bechtel with a shorter body that left 14 frets clear, and soon started making production versions. These were called

Orchestra Models, probably because they were aimed at "orchestra" or big-band guitarists, many of whom were switching from banjo. Martin's catalog of 1930 explains: "Designed especially for plectrum playing in orchestra work. Made only for steel strings." The OMs also had longer scale lengths, banjo-type pegheads (at first) and plastic pickguards.

Despite the OM-style flat-top being designed as a guitar to entice banjo players, it has become recognized as *the* great fingerstyle instrument. The originals did not last long in Martin's line, and are now considered as very desirable collector's items. By 1933 the OM prefix was dropped, because it had become clear how generally useful the new design features were, and aside from the scale length they were incorporated into Martin's regular 000 models.

1930

REGAL ACQUIRES FORMER WASHBURN FACTORY

Regal comes into the front line of Chicago guitar firms in the 1930s when, as well as producing an extensive line under its own name, it makes instruments for many other companies and brands.

◄ **LE DOMINO 4010**

PRODUCED: *c1928-1936*

THIS EXAMPLE: *c1932*

BODY: *13½" wide, 4" deep*

As part of the deal when it took over the defunct Stewart/Washburn factory and its workers in 1930, Regal acquired J.R. Stewart's Le Domino brandname. Regal kept in production some of the existing models, like this suitably decorated guitar, while also introducing at least one new model of its own, the "Big Boy" archtop that appeared in the mid-1930s. Regal continued to sell Le Domino models until around 1937, selling the instruments through a variety of outlets, including Tonk Brothers.

◄ **REGAL 16M ARTIST**

PRODUCED: *c1935-1937*

THIS EXAMPLE: *c1935*

BODY: *14¼" wide, 3½" deep*

Regal was licensed by Dobro to make Dobro-design resonator guitars from 1935. This 16M, for example, is the Regal-brand version of Dobro's own M/16 model (the Dobro is shown on p.43). Regal, based in Chicago, would use Dobro Los Angeles-made bodies, resonators, coverplates and tailpieces. Regal itself made the necks, probably had the engraving and plating done in Chicago, and assembled the instruments. Regals can generally be identified by their distinctive f-holes on the upper body (see left), while Dobros have "windowpane" soundholes. The fancy models (14, 15, 16) lasted only a few years, made by Dobro and Regal; the plainer models (32, 46, 62) were at first only made in L.A. by Dobro, but continued when Regal took over all Dobro production in 1937.

With its roots in Indiana during the first years of the 1900s, Regal was by the 1920s a Chicago-based musical instrument company that made mostly mandolins, although with a nod to the ever-more-popular guitar Regal did in 1927 add to its expanding catalog a line of guitars. These were made for Regal by Stromberg-Voisinet (soon to be renamed Kay).

But it was not until the 1930s that Regal's place in the history of American guitars would become assured.

Two years earlier, Lyon & Healy had sold its Washburn brandname to Tonk, who in turn had hired J. R. Stewart, a small Chicago manufacturer, to take over the Washburn factory and continue making Washburns.

But Stewart went bust, and Tonk began negotiations with Regal. In 1930 Regal took over the defunct Stewart/Washburn factory and began production of Washburns along with a greatly expanded line of Regal models. It was this acquisition of the large, modern Washburn factory and its skilled workers that would help the Regal company to become one of the major guitar manufacturers of the 1930s. A number of the products of Regal's dominant years have been brought together and displayed over these pages.

During the 1930s, as well as building Washburns for Tonk (see p.11-13), Regal made Dobros under license from Dobro, eventually taking over all Dobro production in 1937.

The Chicago company also did contract work for mail-order firms and many other companies and their various brandnames. Regal's activities included the production of guitars and guitar parts for National-Dobro, such as the

◀ **SLINGERLAND CATHEDRANOLA**

PRODUCED: *c1933-1935*

THIS EXAMPLE: *c1934*

BODY: *13½" wide, 3¾" deep*

Henry H. Slingerland started his drum company in Chicago in 1916, and added May Bell and Slingerland brand banjos in the 1920s. Slingerland also had some guitars made by Harmony and Regal in the 1930s. This unusual Regal-made example (left) may look like a resonator guitar, but in fact it features a secondary soundboard suspended inside, not a resonator.

▶ **REGAL ESQUIRE 1185**

PRODUCED: *c1938-1941*

THIS EXAMPLE: *c1939; serial 105*

BODY: *18" wide, 4" deep*

Regal could boast four different archtop "Orchestra Guitars" in its catalog of the late 1930s. These were the $250 Crown 1190, the $125 Esquire 1185 (shown right), the $85 Prince 1170 (shown far right) and the $65 Bob-Cat 1160.

▲ **REGAL PRINCE 1170**

PRODUCED: *c1938-1942*

THIS EXAMPLE: *c1939*

BODY: *18" wide, 4" deep*

Regal described the Prince as having an "ease of action that leaves you unwearied after hours of playing." The guitar's catalog description also mentioned a spruce top and mahogany body, whereas the more expensive Esquire (see left) had a maple body. Later versions of the Prince were sold by the Montgomery Ward mail-order company as its top Recording King model.

bodies and necks it produced for a number of National-Dobro's early electric models. Regal suspended production shortly after America's entry into World War II in 1942. Guitar historian Mike Newton explains: "After the war Regal never really seemed to get going again, and gradually they withered away, eventually going out of business in 1953. The Regal name was later acquired by the Harmony company of Chicago, and beginning in 1959 it was used on a line of student-grade Harmony-made guitars that was marketed by Fender and, consequently, sold by Fender dealers. In recent years, the Regal name has been used by Saga on its imported resonator guitars."

1930

VEGA GOES "ARCHED";
STELLA GOES "12"

Established by two Swedish immigrants in Boston during the earliest years of the 20th century, Vega produces some unusual pressed-and-arched guitars during the 1930s. Meanwhile, the Oscar Schmidt company in Jersey City is more or less alone in meeting most of the as-yet minimal demand for the ringing tones of the flat-top 12-string guitar.

◄ VEGA CREMONA

PRODUCED: *c1930-1933*

THIS EXAMPLE: *c1932; serial 33942*

BODY: *16" wide, 3⅞" deep*

This was the top model in Vega's first archtop series of around 1930, and it used Vega's unusual pressed arched top and back that the company had first used in modified form on earlier mandolins. The Cremona sold for $220 in 1932, compared to a Gibson L-5 at $275. From catalog shots, it appears that the strange twin pickguards are later additions to this rarely seen guitar.

► VEGA CUSTOM

THIS EXAMPLE: *c1936; serial 33942*

BODY: *14¼" wide, 4¼" deep*

This ornately decorated guitar does not appear in any of Vega's instrument catalogs of the period. It seems to have been a custom order, and was given elaborate inlays similar to those found on Vega's high-end banjos of the time.

While Vega's beginnings go back to the 1880s, the company proper began in Boston in 1903 when two Swedish brothers, Julius and Carl Nelson, bought out their other partners, incorporated the company and renamed it Vega (for the brightest star in the constellation of Lyra, which explains the "star" logo often used on Vega instruments).

At first the company concentrated on banjo production, soon buying the Fairbanks operation and in the process acquiring the services of its main man, David L. Day (later of Bacon & Day), who helped establish Vega as a leading light in the banjo world.

As for guitars, Vega probably made small Martin-style parlor instruments from the start, but its main guitar manufacturing period begins around 1930 and uses an

◀ STELLA 12-STRING

PRODUCED: *c1921-1939*

THIS EXAMPLE: *c1930*

BODY: *14⅝" wide, 3⅞" deep*

Stella was one of the in-house brands used by the Oscar Schmidt musical instrument company of Jersey City, New Jersey. Later Stella guitars were sold by Fretted Instrument Manufacturers, who bought the name from Schmidt in 1935 and in turn sold it to Harmony five years later. The Stella 12-string is famous because an F.I.M. version was used by the great bluesman Leadbelly. Twelve-string guitars were not common in the 1930s, but Leadbelly's later "discovery" would lead to a new popularity of the 12-string and to influential 1960s electric models.

▲ VEGA ELECTRIC MANDOLIN

PRODUCED: *c1936-1940*

THIS EXAMPLE: *c1938; serial 38458*

BODY: *9½" wide, 2" deep*

Vega was an early player in the electric string instrument market, and announced its debut electric models in early 1936, soon after Gibson's first offerings. Some of Vega's electrics of the time turn up with "horseshoe"-shape pickups in the style of Rickenbacker. However, based on what can be seen in contemporary catalog shots, as well as on surviving instruments such as this mandolin, Vega appears to have used a variety of quasi-experimental pickups during the exploratory electric period of the mid 1930s.

▲ SAN JOSE ARTIST 12-STRING

PRODUCED: *c1930*

THIS EXAMPLE: *c1930*

BODY: *14½" wide, 4" deep*

This is a version of the Stella 12-string (center guitar on this page) made by Oscar Schmidt for a New York retailer, Horenstein & Sons. It bears a label with the San Jose brand, presumably one of Horenstein's in-house names (which also included Luxor, for banjos).

---

unusual body construction that the Vega company had first applied to mandolins. The mandolin design was patented in 1913 and was known as the "cylinder back" style. It looks like a normal flatback mandolin from the front, but actually has an unusually arched back that is pressed, not carved, and has a raised triangular center section.

Toned down to a slight curving arch, this technique was applied to both the front and back of Vega's early guitars, including models such as the Cremona (shown far left). But these guitars were too expensive for what they offered to the market, and consequently did not sell well.

By the early 1930s Carl Nelson's son William was running the company, and in the summer of 1933 Vega announced its Vegaphone line of five true carved-top f-hole guitars. Guitar

historian Mike Newton: "These were obviously patterned after Epiphone's contemporary line of archtops, and this was the beginning of about 15 years of heavy Epiphone influence on Vega's designs. Some Vega archtop guitars of this period even appear to have used actual Epiphone bodies, coupled with Vega necks. Vega probably figured that they would sell so few of these it would be easier simply to buy bodies from Epiphone rather than tool up to build them themselves."

By the early 1950s Vega began to run out of steam, and the 1960s seem to have been a lean period. In 1970 William Nelson sold Vega to Martin, who wanted to acquire a banjo operation, and in 1980 Martin sold the Vega name to a Korean trading company. More recently the name was bought by Deering, who used it on a Pete Seeger banjo model.

1930

STROMBERG BEGIN MAKING ARCHTOP GUITARS

Elmer Stromberg develops a line of notable handcarved archtop guitars, at first as a minor sideline to his father's general musical instrument business in Boston, Massachusetts. Gradually the quality improves, and in time the Stromberg archtops will come to be recognized as among the finest ever made.

◀ STROMBERG

THIS EXAMPLE: *c1931; serial 324*

BODY: *16½" wide, 3½" deep*

Here's an example of Stromberg's earliest style of guitar, produced during the 1930s. The most distinctive visual feature of the period is the "three-piece" f-hole – meaning a type where the "serifs" at each end are separate from the central element. Later, as seen on the other examples on this page, Stromberg used one-piece f-holes. At such an early stage in the company's guitar development, when Elmer Stromberg made guitars more or less as a sideline, this instrument's label still only refers to Stromberg as a "maker of banjos and drums."

▶ STROMBERG DELUXE

PRODUCED: *c1936-1955*

THIS EXAMPLE: *c1947; serial 578*

BODY: *17¼" wide, 3⅜" deep*

This instrument was made for jazz guitar player Bobby Gibbons, who at one time played with Glenn Miller.

Gibbons' name was suitably engraved by Stromberg on the 15th fret's position marker. The Boston-based Stromberg workshop became a required stopover for jazz guitarists visiting Boston at the time.

◀ STROMBERG DELUXE CUTAWAY

PRODUCED: *c1946-1955*

THIS EXAMPLE: *c1951; serial 600*

BODY: *17¼" wide, 3⅛" deep*

Many collectors have in mind specific instruments that they particularly want to track down, and high on the list for some wealthy huunters are two mighty Stromberg guitars: this blonde Deluxe cutaway; and the blonde Master 400 cutaway (right). These are without doubt the "blue chip" Strombergs, with only a tiny handful of examples in existence.

Stromberg started in business in Boston, Massachusetts, in the very early 1900s. The operation was set up by Charles A. Stromberg, a Swedish immigrant who had arrived in the United States in the late 1880s.

At first the Stromberg company produced banjos and drums. Stromberg's son Elmer, who had been born in Massachusetts in 1895, joined the business at the beginning of the 1910s, and it was Elmer who from the 1930s began to develop the Stromberg guitar line. The instruments that the company produced in the 1940s and 1950s are today among the most highly regarded of all archtop guitars.

Stromberg's early banjos were not of especially notable quality, although the later instruments are much better. By 1927 the Stromberg business had moved within Boston to its

best-known location, 40 Hanover Street, as featured on many Stromberg guitar labels. It was soon after this that Elmer began to produce the first Stromberg guitars.

As with the banjos, the earliest guitar efforts were of unexceptional quality, and it was not until Elmer reorganized and redesigned the guitars in the 1940s that the true potential of the Stromberg line became apparent. Among the changes that Elmer made at that time were a move from three-piece to single-piece f-holes, the adoption of an unusual single diagonal internal bracing system (effectively half a standard X-type), and the addition of a multiple-bound pickguard.

Some body sizes were also increased at this time and later a cutaway option introduced, and Stromberg's two most celebrated models, the Master 300 and Master 400, were

◄ **STROMBERG MASTER 400
CUTAWAY**

PRODUCED: *c1946-1955*

THIS EXAMPLE: *c1952; serial 623*

BODY: *18½" wide, 3¼" deep*

*Strombergs are high quality guitars,
and are quite wonderful instruments
to play. It would seem that Elmer
Stromberg's approach, especially
with the top-of-the-line Master 400
model, was to make an instrument
bigger and louder than anything else
around – in which he seems to have
succeeded. If D'Angelico is a kind of
high-end Gibson, then Stromberg
would be the high-end Epiphone.*

► **STROMBERG G-1**

PRODUCED: *c1936-1955*

THIS EXAMPLE: *c1945; serial 526*

BODY: *17" wide, 3½" deep*

*Although each one was made to
special order, Stromberg guitars
came in six principal models. In
descending order these were the
Master 400, Master 300, Ultra-
Deluxe, Deluxe, G-1 (sometimes
called the G-100) and the G-3.*

launched. Both boasted the largest body – some 19 inches
wide – of any archtop guitar then on the market, including
Gibson's Super 400, D'Angelico's New Yorker and Epiphone's
Emperor, and were designed to offer a concomitantly bigger
sound. Guitar dealer George Gruhn has described such
Strombergs as "the loudest guitars in creation."

The distinctive sound of Strombergs would attract a
number of renowned jazzmen to the instruments, including
players such as Irving Ashby (Nat King Cole, Oscar Peterson)
and Freddie Green (Count Basie). Elmer Stromberg died in
1955, some months after his father, and the Stromberg
business died with them. It's estimated that Stromberg
produced some 640 guitars in total, and today examples that
surface command high prices on the vintage market.

▲ MARTIN D-28

PRODUCED: *1932-current*

THIS EXAMPLE: *1940; serial 74702*

BODY: *15⅝" wide, 4⅞" deep*

At first called the D-2 model by Martin, the D-28 is a modern flat-top guitar classic, a constituent in the trio of that company's great dreadnought instruments, the D-18, the D-28 and the D-45. Players and collectors especially value D-28s from before 1947, which have Martin's distinctive herringbone trim around the top of the guitar's body (and reinstated on the HD-28 that

first appeared in 1976). This exceptional D-28 was acquired from a dealer who in turn had bought it

from the original owner, one Edna Leeper, pictured here with the guitar in her band, The Oklahoma Sweethearts, in about 1941.

► MARTIN F-7

PRODUCED: *1935-1942*

THIS EXAMPLE: *1938; serial 69359*

BODY: *16" wide, 3⅞" deep*

Despite its reputation as the greatest flat-top guitar maker of the time, the Martin company made a number of archtop models during the 1930s, although none survived the war. It's interesting to note that the distinctive hexagonal fingerboard markers of the F series, seen on this F-7, were adopted for the D-45 when that guitar's original "snowflake" markers were dropped in 1939.

1931

MARTIN LAUNCHES THE DREADNOUGHT GUITAR

The classic big-body acoustic flat-top guitar hits the market as Martin unleashes its famous trio of dreadnought guitars, the D-18, D-28 and D-45.

Martin's "dreadnought" guitar design, named for the large, powerful British battleship of the early 20th century, is probably the most famous of Martin's innovations, and like many of the company's designs it would prove to be a great influence on other flat-top guitar makers.

The idea behind the dreadnought design was further to increase the volume, power and tonal versatility of the acoustic flat-top guitar. Martin had first used the new body shape – with a thick waist and wide, square shoulders – for a series of instruments custom built back in the mid-1910s for the Oliver Ditson company, a music publisher and musical instruments retailer with stores in its hometown of Boston as well as in New York and Philadelphia. Martin was making instruments for a number of outside companies during the

first decades of the 1900s, including Paramount (see p.45), Weymann and Wurlitzer as well as Ditson.

The design of the dreadnought has been credited to Harry L. Hunt, who was secretary of the Ditson company and managed its New York store. Hunt, a native of Kansas, worked for Ditson from 1895 to 1930. In 1904 he introduced Lyon & Healy harps on to the market through Ditson, and in 1915 arranged for Martin to make mandolins for Ditson, adding ukuleles and guitars in the following year. Official Martin history says that Hunt "suggested" the dreadnought design as the basis for one of the Martin-Ditson models.

Only a relatively small number of Martin-Ditson guitars was made, but the design was revamped in the early 1930s when Martin was looking for a new, bigger guitar to put on the

▶ MARTIN D-18

PRODUCED: *1932-current*

THIS EXAMPLE: *1935; serial 59670*

BODY: *15⅝″ wide, 4⅝″ deep*

As one plays more and more Martin guitars it becomes apparent that there's a logical method to the company's line of models. The small-body instruments clearly suit more delicate fingerpicking, but as the body gets bigger it lends itself to a more raucous style of music. Martin's big dreadnought, of which the D-18 is the plainest, is the ultimate for hard bluegrass playing and for accompanying singers.

market. Walter Carter writes in *The Martin Book*: "The largest Ditson had been 15⅜″ wide, and in 1931 Martin pulled out the paper pattern (it's still in the Martin archives and it bears the penciled date 7/19/16) and made up some of these big guitars in mahogany and rosewood. Presumably, since these new guitars did not have the body lines of an oversized 000, they received a new designation: D for dreadnought. Although

▼ D'ANGELICO EARLY L-5-STYLE

PRODUCED: *1932-c1936*

THIS EXAMPLE: *c1933; serial 1065*

BODY: *16½″ wide, 3½″ deep*

Every guitar maker has to start somewhere, and for many the best place to begin their studies is by examining and copying the great instruments of the past and present. John D'Angelico was no different in this respect, and with a natural interest

in the archtop "jazz" guitar, he was inevitably drawn in his early years to the design that started the whole genre, Lloyd Loar's classic L-5 guitar (for an original, see pages 30/31). The guitar illustrated here (below) is the first design style that D'Angelico developed, and clearly is a copy of Gibson's L-5. In the view of some observers it's a better guitar, mainly because D'Angelico, working in a small shop, would have taken more care and more time to create an individually pleasing instrument.

▶ D'ANGELICO EXCEL CUTAWAY

PRODUCED: *c1947-1964*

THIS EXAMPLE: *Nov. 1955; serial 1982*

BODY: *17″ wide, 3¼″ deep*

Every D'Angelico instrument seems to have its own personalit: this Excel, for example, has rather more of a refined sound than many. Like virtually every D'Angelico it is a fine guitar – but they're all inevitably different. Note the distinctive "flared" headstock with cupola.

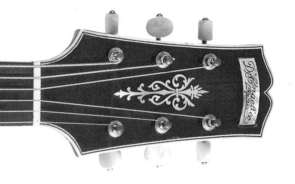

▲ D'ANGELICO NEW YORKER

PRODUCED: *c1936-1964*

THIS EXAMPLE: *Jan. 1960; serial 2100*

BODY: *17¾″ wide, 3″ deep*

The New Yorker was in effect D'Angelico's Super 400, his biggest and most elaborate guitar, with ornate tailpiece and inlays.

begun to define his two most famous models, the New Yorker and the Excel. However, features and appointments were never too precise, and John would adapt and modify as he or his customer chose. During the 1940s and into the 1950s D'Angelico continued to develop his personal style and applied an assured, unique flair for design, gradually adding distinctive decorative touches and subtle improvements to his guitars. All this is demonstrated in the instruments from the collection that are displayed over these three pages. The guitars range from an early 1930s example, that was made very much in the style of Gibson's L-5, to a New Yorker from early in 1960.

D'Angelico stayed in the Kenmare Street premises until 1959 when, after subsidence to his existing shop, he was effectively forced to move to nearby premises. From all accounts D'Angelico was unhappy about the change. DiSerio left around the time of the move, and Jimmy D'Aquisto, who had been working for D'Angelico since the early 1950s, became an increasingly important and valued collaborator. (For more information on and examples of Jimmy D'Aquisto's later work, see pages 108-113.) After repeated heart-related illness in the early 1960s, John D'Angelico died at age 59 in

1932

D'ANGELICO SETS UP NEW YORK SHOP

John D'Angelico establishes the archtop acoustic guitar with his powerful, stylish instruments, made in New York from the early 1930s into the 1960s. While subsequent makers would refine the art of archtop guitars, it was D'Angelico who underlined their tremendous potential, and his fine instruments live on as testament to a great, visionary guitar maker.

◄ GALIANO-CIANI MANDOLIN

THIS EXAMPLE: *c1915*

BODY: *10" wide, 2" deep*

A young John D'Angelico was apprenticed to his grand-uncle Ciani's instrument workshop in N York from around the mid 1910s. This mandolin was made by Rap Ciani for retailer A. Galiano.

John D'Angelico was born in New York City in 1905 into a family that had originally come from Naples, Italy. At age nine D'Angelico was apprenticed to his grand-uncle, Raphael Ciani, who ran a workshop on Kenmare Street, New York, making and repairing various string instruments including violins, mandolins and guitars. At this time, John also began to study violin making and playing with a local man, Mario Frosali.

In his teens D'Angelico came to run the Ciani business after his grand-uncle died, but in 1932 John decided to set out independently, and he started his own shop a few doors along in Kenmare Street (also renting an apartment above the shop). It was in the Kenmare Street shop that the majority of D'Angelico's legendary guitars were created. John's assistant,

Vincent ('Jimmy') DiSerio, had first started working D'Angelico's shop age 12 back in 1932 as an odd-job boy, from the mid-1940s DiSerio became an increasi important part of the instrument building, which inclu guitars, mandolins and, reportedly, violins.

At first when D'Angelico set up on his own in the e 1930s he began to make archtop guitars in the style of industry-standard Gibson L-5 of the period. Instruments this type were designed primarily for accompaniment, usu intended to be played with some kind of dance band. But s John began to make his own mark and started refining instruments, and jazz players in particular began to use th for solo work, drawn to D'Angelico's big, powerful guitars their distinctive sound and presence. By 1936 D'Angelico

▼ DITSON STYLE 1-45

PRODUCED: *c1920*

THIS EXAMPLE: *c1920; serial 463*

BODY: *11⅛" wide, 3⅞" deep*

Oliver Ditson started his music publishing and musical instrument retail business in Boston,

Massachusetts, at least as far back as the 1860s. Gradually, Ditson added stores in New York and Philadelphia to expand his business beyond Boston, and in 1864 Ditson founded Lyon & Healy as his Chicago branch. (Lyon & Healy split from Ditson and was operating independently by 1880.) Harry L.

Hunt joined the Ditson organization in 1895 and, as well as managing the company's New York store, he was instrumental in arranging for outside manufacturers to build instruments for Ditson, including Martin. Among the rare Martin-Ditson guitars is this beautiful small body model, known as Style 1-45.

▲ DITSON "DREADNOUGHT"

PRODUCED: *1916-1921, 1923-1930*

THIS EXAMPLE: *1924; serial 21539*

BODY: *15⅞" wide, 4⅝" deep*

If Martin had not conceived the dreadnought guitar, then it's quite possible that music as we know it

might have been totally different, because the dreadnought opened up a new tonality and volume to guitar players. It also gave access to a different side of the musician's personality. This rare Ditson was the first outing for the "12-fret" dreadnought style, later popularized in Martin's own "14-fret" versions.

dreadnought guitars were essentially Styles 18 and 28, first examples were stamped D-1 and D-2. In 1932 the [mo]del names were changed to D-18 and D-28."

[Th]ese first dreadnoughts had a neck that joined the body [at t]he 12th fret (as had the Ditsons), but starting in 1934, [follo]wing the success of its 14th-fret-join OM models, Martin [gav]e the new D models a 14-fret neck and a necessarily [som]ewhat shorter body. The Martin dreadnought had arrived.

[A]t first the dreadnoughts were advertised as "bass [gui]tars," but were completely different to the modern notion [of a] bass guitar. With the extra air volume inside the larger, [deep]er body, the dreadnought style offered a much rounder and [fulle]r bass presence, suiting bass-heavy accompaniment in [stri]ng-instrument ensembles or to singing. It was in the latter

category, especially in country and bluegrass, that the dreadnought would find an especially accordant place.

Martin created a classic of modern American guitar making when they applied their finest decorative style, 45, to the new dreadnought size in 1933. Singing cowboy star Gene Autry ordered the first such instrument from the company, and between 1933 and 1942 (when the model was dropped in the wake of World War II) Martin made 91 D-45s. The model was reintroduced in 1968 and is still in production today.

Other makers joined Martin in producing similar fat-waisted body styles at the time. But although Martin's dreadnought guitars proved less than popular when first introduced, they have since become established as one of the great designs of the modern American acoustic instrument.

▲ MARTIN D-45

PRODUCED: *1933-1942, 1968-cur[rent]*

THIS EXAMPLE: *1941; serial 7706[...]*

BODY: *15½" wide, 4⅝" deep*

Only 91 pre-war D-45s wer[e made] and in the view of many pla[yers and] collectors they are among t[he] highest quality, best soundin[g...] ever made. With so few in ex[istence] and with such wide knowledg[e of] their almost magical quality, [these] superb, rare and inevitably e[xpensive] instruments appear to follow [no] rules of supply and demand [...]

▼ D'ANGELICO NEW YORKER

PRODUCED: *c1936-1964*

THIS EXAMPLE: *Dec. 1953; serial 1909*

BODY: *18" wide, 3½" deep*

Jimmy D'Aquisto worked with John D'Angelico in the D'Angelico workshop from the early 1950s, and for those who knew D'Aquisto he was a great source of information on D'Angelico and his guitars. One of the stories D'Aquisto used to tell related to the fantastic art deco

elements that are featured on many of D'Angelico's instruments. For the inlay on the peghead of the New Yorker, for instance, D'Aquisto said that one day John was looking out of the window of his shop at the Chrysler building in New York, and that's what inspired the design. This particular New Yorker (below) is a very rare left-handed example. Of course, very few players ordered left-hand models, and the company ledgers reveal that this one was made for one Al Gareffa.

▲ D'ANGELICO EXCEL CUTAWAY

PRODUCED: *c1947-1964*

THIS EXAMPLE: *Mar. 1950; serial 1835*

BODY: *17" wide, 3½" deep*

The Excel was an extension of John D'Angelico's interest in the Gibson L-5 guitar, but overlaid with his own character and his own ideas.

September 1964. A brief obituary that appeared in *The New York Times* described D'Angelico as a "short, modest and cheerful man," and noted pithily that, despite building and repairing mandolins and violins, "the making of fine guitars was his obsession."

John D'Angelico had an incredible sense of aesthetics, and the guitars he made are beautiful, both as works of art and as musical instruments. (For an unusual example of D'Angelico's custom work, see page 96.) According to surviving records published in Akira Tsumura's *Guitars – The Tsumura Collection* and ranging from November 1932 to January 1961, D'Angelico made a total of 1,164 numbered guitars. Today they are widely sought by players and collectors alike, and are among the most highly valued guitars ever produced.

▲ D'ANGELICO NEW YORKER

PRODUCED: *c1936-1964*

THIS EXAMPLE: *May 1939; serial 1411*

BODY: *17¾" wide, 3½" deep*

Here is an early, non-cutaway example of D'Angelico's New Yorker model. According to the records it was made for one Joe Senacorin.

▶ D'ANGELICO MANDOLIN

PRODUCED: *c1935-1964*

THIS EXAMPLE: *May 1941; serial 141*

BODY: *10¼" wide, 2⅛" deep*

While it is clear that these two mandolins are based on Gibson designs, the top example has the distinctive D'Angelico headstock with its "cupola" decoration at the very tip. In fact, this mandolin is noted in the D'Angelico ledger as "G.D.", and we must presume that these are the original owner's initials.

▲ D'ANGELICO MANDOLIN

PRODUCED: *c1935-1964*

THIS EXAMPLE: *c1938; serial 115*

BODY: *10½" wide, 2¼" deep*

Some rate the mandolins that D'Angelico made as top quality instruments, even if the designs themselves may not be too original.

▲ D'ANGELICO SPECIAL

THIS EXAMPLE: *Jan. 1949; serial 1807*

BODY: *18¾" wide, 3⅝" deep*

With a body that is close on 19 inches wide, this unusual D'Angelico guitar with its oval soundhole is as far as is known the biggest one that D'A made. It is also one of the most powerful sounding instruments that you'll ever hear. One player described it as like thunder coming out of a soundhole, and it's certainly not refined or pretty at all – just massive. It's unlikely D'Angelico would make a guitar without f-holes unless the customer – in this case one F. Orlando – requested it.

▶ D'ANGELICO SPECIAL

THIS EXAMPLE: *Oct. 1941; serial 1551*

BODY: *17" wide, 3¼" deep*

This is thought to be the only guitar that John D'Angelico ever made in mahogany. As a result, it constitutes a distinct departure from the classic

D'Angelico sound, and is markedly different when compared to the regular maple-body D'Angelico guitars, sounding perhaps lighter and more "open." Many feel that maple produces a higher quality sound, and so it is perhaps understandable that D'A made only this one mahogany example.

▶ D'ANGELICO ELECTRIC

THIS EXAMPLE: *c1960*

BODY: *16¾" wide, 3½" deep*

The high quality body suggests that it may have been D'Angelico-made, which would make it a rarity among the "bought-in body" electrics.

▼ D'ANGELICO ELECTRIC

THIS EXAMPLE: *c1955*

BODY: *16¾" wide, 2¾" deep*

It seems that John D'Angelico must have viewed the electric guitars he sold as quite apart from his main business of producing superb

acoustic archtop instruments. This we can deduce from the fact that most of the plywood bodies for the electrics (assembled apparently purely to fill market demand) were bought in by D'Angelico from outside suppliers, from either United Guitars or Codé. Both of these operations were based in nearby New Jersey.

▼ D'ANGELICO ELECTRIC LEFT

THIS EXAMPLE: *c1955*

BODY: *16½" wide, 2½" deep*

This is another of the electric guitars that D'Angelico made using a plywood body that he bought in from an outside supplier – although the

necks on these "sideline" guitars were in fact made in the D'Angelico workshop. Perhaps he considered the electric models as quasi-mass production, entry-level D'Angelico instruments. No doubt there would as usual have been fewer left-hand examples produced than the regular right-hand guitars.

D'Angelico will always be noted among the top handful of makers of the carved-top f-hole acoustic guitar. But as we demonstrate on these two pages, alongside his better-known lines he also made a number of mandolins, electric guitars, instruments without f-holes, and experimental guitars.

The surviving D'Angelico ledgers, where the instrument sales were noted, reveal that, especially in the earlier days, the customer was often a music store: New York outlets such as Silver & Horland, Fordham, Gravois and Manny's all appear in the listings. But the number of top-flight players who would come to visit with D'Angelico and talk guitars and guitar making – and order guitars – began to increase as the D'Angelico name and reputation spread. Oscar Moore ordered a couple of Excels from D'Angelico in the 1940s while with

Nat King Cole, and George Shearing's guitarist Chuck Wayne also went for an Excel. Johnny Smith was a famous D'Angelico player during the 1950s, and New York session supremo Mundell Lowe had at least two Excels direct from the workshop at that time – he may even have bumped into Chet Atkins leaving with a New Yorker Cutaway. Mel Bay bought a New Yorker in the 1950s and featured it prominently on the covers of many of his popular guitar method books.

As Paul Schmidt wrote in *Acquired Of The Angels*: "John D'Angelico left himself to the world in the form of his instruments, for each one testifies to some element of his personality, his character, his artistry and his soul."

1933

GRETSCH INTRODUCES OWN-BRAND GUITARS

Fifty years after its founding in New York City, the Fred Gretsch Manufacturing Company finally issues guitars under its own name in the early 1930s. Musicians and salespeople are telling the company that the guitar is quickly replacing the banjo to become the leading string instrument of the day, and commercial wisdom prevails. Later in the 1930s Gretsch would issue its most stylish archtop line, the beautiful Synchromatics.

▼ GRETSCH SYNCHROMATIC 400

PRODUCED: *c1939-1955 (also 6040/6041)*

THIS EXAMPLE: *c1945; serial 339*

BODY: *18" wide, 3½" deep*

The 400 was top of the five Synchromatics introduced by Gretsch in 1939, alongside the 300, 200 and 160 models. The big 18-inch body of the 400 and the long 26-inch scale of all five original Synchromatic models meant that they must have been designed to be powerful, gutsy instruments, and the 400 was intended to compete with Gibson's Super 400 and D'Angelico's New Yorker.

▲ GRETSCH RHUMBA

PRODUCED: *c1933-1935*

THIS EXAMPLE: *c1933*

BODY: *16" wide, 3¼" deep*

The round body of this strange, shortlived instrument was presumably meant to entice banjo players to the newly popular guitar.

The Fred Gretsch Manufacturing Co. was established in 1883 when a German immigrant, Friedrich Gretsch, left the employ of a small New York banjo and drum maker, Houdlett, to set up on his own. Soon Gretsch was producing a line of drums, banjos, tambourines and novelty toy instruments from his new firm's humble premises in Brooklyn, selling to local musical instrument wholesalers such as Bruno or Wurlitzer.

When Friedrich died suddenly in 1895 his son Fred took over the business, and by 1900 had added mandolins to the lines produced by the company. In 1916 business was good enough to complete construction of a large ten-story Gretsch building close to the Brooklyn side of the Williamsburg Bridge

▲ **GRETSCH RANCHER**

PRODUCED: *c1954-1980, 1989-current*

THIS EXAMPLE: *c1955; serial 16172*

BODY: *16¾" wide, 4⅛" deep*

The Rancher was in effect an acoustic flat-top version of Gretsch's new Western guitars that were

introduced in the mid-1950s. These included the solidbody Round-Up and the electric Chet Atkins Hollow Body model. Like those, the Rancher had a big G (for Gretsch) "branded" into the top of the body, and Western motifs such as cacti and steer's heads engraved into the pearl-block fingerboard markers.

◄ **GRETSCH SYNCHROMATIC 6031 TENOR**

PRODUCED: *c1951-1955*

THIS EXAMPLE: *c1954; serial 11230*

BODY: *17" wide, 3½" deep*

The Gretsch Synchromatic appeared with a cutaway body during the early 1950s and was available in

sunburst (called model 6030) or natural finish (model 6031), although Gretsch renamed these as the Constellation later in the decade. The tenor version shown here was in fact a rare option. Tenor guitars were designed to suit the musician more used to tenor banjos but who wished to double occasionally on guitar.

▲ **GRETSCH SYNCHROMATIC CUSTOM**

THIS EXAMPLE: *c1953; serial 7712*

BODY: *17" wide, 3½" deep*

Gretsch guitars are renowned among collectors for wild inconsistency in the way that design features were implemented on particular models. Instruments that defy catalog descriptions, such as the guitar shown, are regularly encountered. Despite 6030-like appointments, it has the gold-bound soundholes more familiar from the Synchromatic 400.

that crossed the East River to Manhattan. By the early 1920s Gretsch was advertising an enormous and flourishing line of instruments, primarily with the Rex and 20th Century brandnames and including banjos, mandolins, guitars, violins, band instruments, drums, bells, accordions, harmonicas, phonographs and a wide variety of accessories that included items such as strings, cases and stands.

As the guitar began to replace the banjo in general popularity at the end of the 1920s and into the 1930s, Gretsch for the first time started to use its own name as a brand for guitars, around 1933. These new Gretsch guitars included the unusual Rhumba (far left), as well as the American Orchestra series of archtop acoustic instruments and a number of flat-tops such as the Broadkaster model. The distinctive, stylish Synchromatic line appeared in 1939. With various changes of style and name, some of the Synchromatic designs would stay in the Gretsch line for ten or more years, into the mid-1950s.

Gretsch's 1939 catalog extolled the new line's virtues with what it called "seven points of supremacy": the new "non-pressure" asymmetrical neck; the "synchronized" bridge; "chromatic" tailpiece; large carved-top body; "streamlined" cat's eye soundholes; "perfect finish"; and an "ironclad guarantee." Popular guitarist Harry Volpe, Gretsch's leading endorser of the day, was quoted as saying: "My fingers seem to travel twice as fast on my new Synchromatic."

1934

GIBSON'S FIRST JUMBO FLAT-TOPS ANNOUNCED

Necessarily responsive to the needs of musicians and to developments made by other makers, Gibson reacts to players' calls for bigger guitars and to Martin's introduction of big dreadnought models.

◄ **GIBSON SJ-200**

PRODUCED: *1938-current (also as J-200)*

THIS EXAMPLE: *Mar. 1954; serial A16742*

BODY: *17" wide, 4½" deep*

The leading guitar among Gibson's "narrow waist" jumbos is this famous model, known variously during its long and distinguished career as the Super Jumbo, SJ-200 or J-200.

▼ **GIBSON JUMBO CUSTOM**

THIS EXAMPLE: *c1935; serial 201A*

BODY: *15⅞" wide, 4½" deep*

This unusual one-off custom-ordered guitar was effectively a fancy Jumbo model. It coupled the early Jumbo body with a neck and pickguard more often seen on Gibson's L-7.

▲ **MARTELLE DELUXE**

THIS EXAMPLE: *c1935; serial 0062*

BODY: *16" wide, 4¾" deep*

Here is another rare and unusual custom variant of Gibson's earliest Jumbo model, probably made soon after the Jumbo's introduction in 1934. This guitar may have been produced especially for a musical instruments retailer called Martelle or, perhaps more likely given the extreme rarity of examples, for an individual named Martelle.

▲ GIBSON SJ-100

PRODUCED: *1939-1943*

THIS EXAMPLE: *Dec. 1939; serial EA-5634*

BODY: *16¾" wide, 4¼" deep*

This mahogany-body version of the rosewood J-200 was visually distinct from its more expensive cousin

thanks to the peghead that had distinctive "stair-step"-shape sides for its first few years of production, as well as a different pickguard. Its J-200-like "mustache" bridge was also replaced after the J-100's first couple of years of production. Gibson chose not to reintroduce the slow-selling J-100 after the war.

◄ GIBSON SUPER JUMBO

PRODUCED: *1938-current (also as SJ/J-200)*

THIS EXAMPLE: *1938*

BODY: *16¾" wide, 4½" deep*

Two of Hollywood's earliest singing cowboys, Ray "Crash" Corrigan and Ray Whitley, suggested ideas to Gibson that resulted in the Super Jumbo model. The new narrow-waist flat-top jumbo shape was borrowed from Gibson's newly enlarged archtop L-5 guitar – which had been offered with the "Advanced" 17-inch

wide body from 1934 – and would go on to fame under its soon-official model name of J-200. The 200 flaunted its high-end status: just look at those large and ornate pearl markers flanking the fingerboard, the multiple binding outlining body and neck, the flowering vines of the pickguard, and the outrageously elaborate "mustache" bridge that is shaped like nothing less than a pair of cow's horns. No wonder that the flamboyant 200 was described for years in Gibson literature as "The King of the Flat-top Guitars."

▲ GIBSON ADVANCED JUMBO

PRODUCED: *c1936-1940, 1990-current*

THIS EXAMPLE: *c1938*

BODY: *15¾" wide, 4½" deep*

In the mid-1930s, "Advanced" meant "big" at Gibson. The company enlarged the size of many of its archtop guitars at this time, and at the same time introduced two great new instruments, the Advanced Jumbo and the Super 400, which defined the art of flat-top and archtop guitar making.

Gibson reacted to Martin's earlier introduction of the large dreadnought D-series flat-tops (see p.52) by issuing its biggest flat-top in 1934, the aptly named Gibson Jumbo model. Echoing the sales points of the new Martins, Gibson's launch-year catalog assured its prospective customers that the just-out Jumbo model "produces a heavy, booming tone so popular with many players who do vocal or small combination accompaniment."

The essential design of that earliest Gibson Jumbo would live on in the company's lines for decades to come, and is still in production today. Especially popular have been the fine models of the "J" series such as the J-45, used by many distinguished players through the years from flatpicking guru Doc Watson to the songwriting Buddy Holly. Many players and

collectors put special value on the Advanced Jumbo model, made for a relatively short time during the late-1930s. Eldon Whitford and his co-authors said in *Gibson's Fabulous Flat-Top Guitars*: "If you're lucky enough to play one of these pre-war creations, be prepared for attitude readjustment and brain alteration. The Advanced Jumbo becomes the frame of reference for every other flat-top you will ever play."

Gibson's other notable style of jumbo flat-top was the "narrow waist" design, exemplified by the Super Jumbo models introduced at the very end of the 1930s and still known today in their most popular manifestation, the J-200. This has fired the music of a host of musicians, ranging from co-designer and singing cowboy Ray Whitley to country-bluesman Rev. Gary Davis and country star Emmylou Harris.

1934

GIBSON'S FINEST ARCHTOP, THE SUPER 400, IS LAUNCHED

Gibson reacts to the lean years of the Depression of the early 1930s by concentrating on production of cheap wooden toys rather than expensive guitars. However, in 1934 Gibson completely revamps its acoustic archtop lines, producing the improved "Advanced" models and introducing the greatest of its archtops, the prime Super 400.

▲ **GIBSON SUPER 400**

PRODUCED: *1934-1942, 1948-1955*

THIS EXAMPLE: *1942; serial 97505*

BODY: *18" wide, 3⅜" deep*

From 1937 Gibson widened the upper bout of the Super 400 by almost an inch and a quarter, and while at first the company continued to apply X-bracing to the underside of the top, by 1940 Gibson had moved to parallel-bracing, which provided a rather more open sound that suited the archtop design. World War II halted production of most guitars, including the Super 400, in 1942. According to the company's surviving shipping records, by that time Gibson had made 408 non-cutaway Super 400s (401 in sunburst and just seven in natural), along with 47 cutaway "Premiere" Super 400s (comprising 29 in sunburst and 18 in natural).

Gibson's brand new Super 400 model of 1934 was a spectacular no-holds-barred guitar, bigger, better and more flashy than any archtop being made by any other manufacturer at the time. After virtually suspending guitar production in the early 1930s, Gibson came on in grand style in 1934, improving its four f-hole archtops of the time, the L-5, L-7, L-10 and L-12, from their existing 16-inch wide body to the new 17-inch "Advanced" body. And Gibson figured that yet another inch was more than justified in order for the company to establish its new 18-inch deluxe archtop – the luxurious, upscale Super 400 – as the clear market leader in its field. Gibson did not hesitate when it came to announcing the fabulous new

► GIBSON SUPER 400 PREMIERE NE

THIS EXAMPLE: *c1940; serial 96014*

BODY: *18" wide, 3½" deep*

Evidence that Gibson was trying out the idea of an electric Super 400

well in advance of the Super 400CES model of 1951 (see p.77), this custom order one-off instrument has the slant-mounted pickup that Gibson was applying at the time to models such as the ES-300.

▼ GIBSON SUPER 400 PREMIERE N

PRODUCED: *1939-1942, 1950-1983 (400C)*

THIS EXAMPLE: *1939; serial EA5341*

BODY: *18" wide, 3½" deep*

This is a very important instrument: Gibson's Super 400 was its finest

archtop, and this one was made in the first year it came with a cutaway. It is without question the rarest and most desirable Super 400 illustrated in this book, and is today an extremely valuable instrument. It represents Gibson's attempt at the time to make the best-ever guitar.

◄ GIBSON SUPER 400

PRODUCED: *1934-1942, 1948-1955*

THIS EXAMPLE: *1934; serial 92093*

BODY: *18" wide, 3½" deep*

It is said that this is the very first Super 400 that Gibson made. It was built especially for a jazz guitarist

called Muzzy Marcellino (note the "Muzzy" on the peghead inlay and "MM" on the truss-rod cover), and

the floating twin "McCarty" pickup is of the type that Marcellino added to the acoustic instrument in his later career (see picture below, center). This first-year Super 400 shows how the model started life bursting with luxurious features, but with a relatively narrow upper bout (the part above the body's "waist"). The upper bout of the Super 400 was in fact widened around 1937

(compare this guitar with the post-'36 400s on these pages, all of which have the later, wider upper bout). Other decorative touches added to early Super 400s included the stylish echo of the "slashed-diamond" inlay on the rear of the peghead (shown here, inset), and the ornate script "Super 400" that from about 1937 was engraved onto the ivory heel cap at the instrument's neck/body join (shown left). This exceptional guitar marks the start of Gibson's supreme archtop achievement.

Muzzy Marcellino (seen above with guitar in Gibson's 1960 catalog) ordered one of the first Super 400s from Gibson in 1934. At the time he was playing with West Coast bandleader Ted Fio Rito, a Hammond organist whose band of the 1930s included future film star Betty Grable on vocals.

instrument. "Every decade has its outstanding creations – a great and inspired leader, an amazing invention, an awe inspiring building, a record smashing horse," trumpeted the company's copywriter in a special Super 400 brochure. "Their originality, character, finesse and inherent quality place them far above the ordinary – an inspiration to all but never duplicated in every measure.

"The Super 400 is an extraordinary guitar in every way – its price is a criterion of its quality," continued the 1934 brochure, offering the new luxury model for a distinctly luxurious $400. This was in the midst of a sweeping economic depression, when Gibson's next guitar on its pricelist was the L-5 at $275, and Gibson's competitor Epiphone's most expensive archtop was the DeLuxe, also at $275. So the

Super 400 had to exude class from tip to toe. The enlarged peghead had a glorious "slashed diamond" inlay; the rich ebony fingerboard boasted elaborate "slashed block" markers; the huge body had no fewer than seven layers of binding at its edges; the massive engraved tailpiece was at once impressive and imposing; and Gibson employed a special layering method to achieve the pickguard's stylish "marbleized" tortoiseshell effect.

Bruce Nixon aptly described the instrument in the introduction to Thomas A. Van Hoose's exhaustive study, *The Gibson Super 400 – Art Of The Fine Guitar*: "The Super 400 has established itself as one of the great aristocrats of the instrument, a guitar whose elegance and purposefulness are obvious even to people who do not play the guitar."

▲ GIBSON SUPER 400CN-WAL

THIS EXAMPLE: *Dec. 1969; serial 844908*

BODY: *18" wide, 3½" deep*

From the front this looks to be a normal, very nice Super 400. It is fitted with a "floating" pickup, a unit that is designed to amplify the guitar without interfering with the natural resonance of the top. Overall, it appears a pristine

example of a natural-finish Super 400 of the 1960s. However, a look at the back of this guitar (below) reveals an unusually dark color compared to the normal yellow maple tones of back and sides. The instrument's label says that it is a "S-400CN WAL," and in fact the guitar's back and sides are maple with a dark stain, possibly walnut (hence the "WAL"). At least one other example is noted in the company's records for late 1969.

Gibson reintroduced the Super 400 during the late 1940s and early 1950s following the break in production caused by the United States' involvement in World War II. It was in 1948 that production of the non-cutaway type recommenced, while the cutaway type reappeared during 1950. This latter variety was officially renamed as the Super 400 Cut-away, usually shortened to "Super 400C," effectively replacing the pre-war designation of Premiere for cutaway models.

The two post-war Super 400s from the collection shown on these pages are not normal production models. Special one-off custom orders were available from Gibson's original factory in Kalamazoo, Michigan, from its earliest days, but a proper Custom Department was not officially established until the 1960s. Later, from 1983 to 1988, there would be a

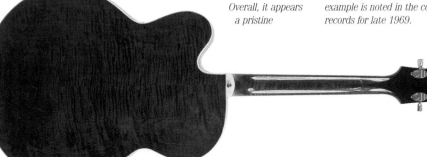

▲ GIBSON SUPER 300

PRODUCED: 1948-1955

THIS EXAMPLE: Apr. 1952; serial A10267

BODY: 18" wide, 3½" deep

Introduced at the same time that the Super 400 reappeared again after World War II, Gibson's Super 300

model had an 18-inch wide body like the Super 400, but was available at a less expensive price. It also bore the 400's ornate tailpiece, but otherwise had many of the features of Gibson's L-7 acoustic archtop of the period, such as the "double parallelogram" fingerboard inlays and the "crown" peghead inlay.

▼ GIBSON SUPER 300C

PRODUCED: 1954-1958

THIS EXAMPLE: Apr. 1957; serial A25494

BODY: 18" wide, 3¼" deep

Once Gibson began to reestablish its acoustic archtop models after World War II, cutaway versions appeared later than

non-cutaway models. The Super 300, for example, was launched without cutaway in 1948, but a cutaway option was not offered until the mid-1950s. From its inception in 1948 until it was dropped in 1958, the combined cutaway and non-cutaway production of Super 300s was just over 200 units, compared to nearly twice that number of Super 400 models during the same period.

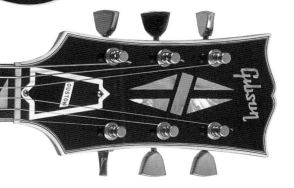

▼ GIBSON SUPER 400C-WR

PRODUCED: 1976-1980

THIS EXAMPLE: 1977; serial 06 103654

BODY: 17¾" wide, 3½" deep

Normally, the Super 400 has been available only in sunburst or natural finishes, but in the late 1970s Gibson

offered two further color options. These were the wine red of the example shown here, as well as ebony. These relatively solid colors were instituted to use up stocks of plainer wood that was less suitable for use with natural or sunburst where the lack of grain and figure would be more evident.

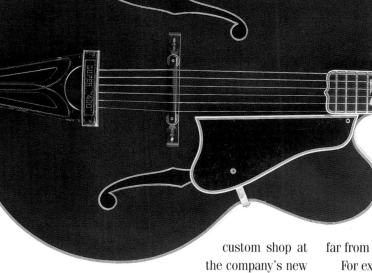

custom shop at the company's new Nashville plant, which opened in summer 1975. The Nashville custom shop would open again in 1992, effectively as two operations: one, building artists' guitars, was coupled with R&D (research and development, which instigates new models); the other made custom orders for retailers.

Also shown here, at the top of this page, are two examples of Gibson's Super 300. The non-cutaway version of this new model was introduced in 1948, at the same time as the return

of the Super 400. In effect the Super 300 offered guitarists the chance to acquire the desirably big 18-inch body of the Super 400, but at a more affordable price. In fact, the Super 300 was not far from being half the price of a Super 400.

For example, the company's June 1949 pricelist offered no less than eight acoustic archtop guitars. There were the two 18-inch models, the Super 400 selling for $425 in sunburst and $450 in natural, and the Super 300 at $250 (sunburst only). Then came Gibson's three 17-inch models, the L-5 at $375 ($390 in natural), the sunburst L-12 at $250, and the $175 L-7 ($190 in natural). Finally, the 1949 pricelist shows the 16-inch guitars: the L-4, available at $135 ($145 natural), the L-50 at $95, and the humble L-48 for $75.

▶ RICKENBACKER SPANISH (SP)

PRODUCED: *1946-1950*

THIS EXAMPLE: *c1947; serial 1005*

BODY: *16" wide, 3⅜" deep*

Rickenbacker's early expertise lay in metals and plastics, so wooden bodies were bought from Harmony of Chicago for this early electric. Note the distinctive "horseshoe" pickup.

◀ RICKENBACKER ELECTRO SPANISH

PRODUCED: *1935-1942 (also Model B)*

THIS EXAMPLE: *c1937; serial B517*

BODY: *9¼" wide, 1¾" deep*

George Beauchamp was probably responsible for the introduction of the Electro Spanish, arguably the first "solidbody" electric guitar. It was molded from Bakelite, the first synthetic plastic. The body did have tiny pockets under the thick, solid top, but these were intended to reduce weight rather than to add any acoustic resonance.

1935

RICKENBACKER ADDS ELECTRICS; EPIPHONE LAUNCHES THE EMPEROR

Rickenbacker builds on its reputation as one of the earliest companies in the electric guitar business by offering a new "solidbody" Bakelite instrument and a wooden body electric. At the same time, Epiphone plays one-upmanship with Gibson by introducing an archtop that is bigger than the new Super 400.

▲ EPIPHONE ZEPHYR

PRODUCED: *1939-1942 (this style)*

THIS EXAMPLE: *c1941; serial 7060*

BODY: *16½" wide, 3½" deep*

Epiphone was an early entrant in the electric guitar business, issuing its

Electraphone and then Electar models in the mid-1930s, while Epiphone's Master pickup of 1937, designed by Herb Sunshine, was the first with individually adjustable polepieces. The Zephyr was one of three Spanish electrics of the time, alongside the Century and Coronet.

▶ EPIPHONE EMPEROR CUTAWAY

PRODUCED: *c1950-1970*

THIS EXAMPLE: *1954; serial 68907*

BODY: *18¼" wide, 3½" deep*

Natural guitars, said Epiphone, had "a handrubbed finish in which the beautiful grain of the selected wood is the decorative motif."

◀ EPIPHONE EMPEROR

PRODUCED: *1935-c1955*

THIS EXAMPLE: *c1948*

BODY: *18" wide, 3⅜" deep*

A beautiful example of the natural-finish Emperor, this is especially important because it was owned by Frixo Stathopoulo. He was one of the three sons of Epiphone founder Anastasios Stathopoulo. His brother Epi took over the company in 1915 when their father died. Frixo (1905-1957) became treasurer, and later vice-president after Epi died, soon selling his interest to brother Orphie.

Frixo is seen playing this guitar with various family members (below). This was his personal guitar, and the

relativewho once owned it said that Frixo "scoured the earth" to find the best materials. The wood is superb (see also the back, above left), and it's a wonderful guitar to play.

▼ EPIPHONE EMPEROR

PRODUCED: *1935-c1955*

THIS EXAMPLE: *1949; serial 58092*

BODY: *18⅛" wide, 3⅜" deep*

A fine sunburst Emperor from Epiphone's New York production period, which ended in 1953 when the factory moved to Philadelphia.

Rickenbacker had produced one of the first electric guitars, in 1931, the prototype "Frying Pan" that led to production versions from summer 1932. This was a lap steel guitar with a long neck and round body (hence the nickname), and a "horseshoe" shape pickup developed by George Beauchamp.

Rickenbacker had its beginnings in Swiss immigrant Adolph Rickenbacker's Los Angeles tool-and-die company, which supplied metal parts to nearby National. Rickenbacker, Beauchamp and Paul Barth formed Ro-Pat-In late in 1931 to produce the Frying Pan, and three years later changed the company name to the Electro String Instrument Corporation, producing further electric guitars up to World War II.

Meanwhile, on the East Coast, Epiphone reacted very quickly to Gibson's introduction of its 18-inch-body Super 400

model. The New York-based Epiphone operation went half an inch better with its large new archtop model of 1935, the Emperor. As we have already discovered (see p.33-35) Epiphone's roots were in banjo making. But Epiphone was one of the few banjo companies that correctly forecasted and, more importantly, acted on the downfall of that instrument during the late 1920s and the subsequent rise of the guitar.

Epiphone had made the Recording series of guitars in the late 1920s, and then the Masterbilt line, but the Emperor of 1935 was by far the company's most prestigious model, with a name taken from the top model of its old Recording banjos. Epiphone's catalog of the time described the new Emperor guitar as "handicraft at its finest" and, to make the point clear to Gibson fans, "The Emperor is the largest guitar made."

▲ WILKANOWSKI

PRODUCED: *c1939-1940*

THIS EXAMPLE: *c1940; serial 6462*

BODY: *15¾" wide, 3½" deep*

The violin theme was echoed in the shape of the pickguard and the peghead, the latter possibly an influence on modern Ovation design.

1939

*WILKANOWSKI MAKES
VIOLIN SHAPE GUITARS*

*A Polish immigrant violin maker,
Willi Wilkanowski produces a
handful of violin-influenced
archtop guitars.*

Wilkanowski guitars are among the most unusual acoustic instruments produced in the United States during the last 60 years. These rare archtop, f-hole guitars resemble nothing less than violin-family instruments, drawing on Wilkanowski's main business as a maker of violins and violas.

Very little is known about Willi Wilkanowski, but the following can be deduced from the few facts available. Wilkanowski was born in Poland in March 1886, and started to make violins as a youngster – he made his first instrument at age nine. Around 1920 he emigrated to the U.S. and went to work making violins for the Oliver Ditson company in Boston, with whom he was associated until the late 1930s. Around 1938 he moved to New York and made violins for Fred Gretsch Manufacturing, and set up on his own in Brooklyn

around 1939, which is when his few guitars were made. He also started making violins and violas for the New York Board of Education at this point, and seems to have continued to work in his own right into the 1950s.

Wilkanowski is thought to have died in New York around 1960. One estimate has put his output until 1941 at 5,000 violins, 100 violas and 30 guitars, although of course no official production figures exist. Wilkanowski's instruments are generally regarded as being of good craftsmanship, and the guitars, as can be seen from the examples shown here, are certainly interesting in design and execution.

The only information given away by the two Wilkanowski guitars shown in this book which include labels is that the operation is described as "Wilkanowski & Son" (which is not

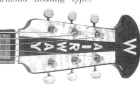

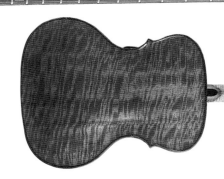

▼ WILKANOWSKI AIRWAY

PRODUCED: *c1939-1940*

THIS EXAMPLE: *1940*

BODY: *17" wide, 3½" deep*

A refined example of Wilkanowski's rare guitar work (note the beautiful back, below), with a streamlined soundhole and wooden tailpiece that would not look out of place among some modern archtop guitars. The inside back of this instrument is signed "W. Wilkanowski 1939" and the label dated 1940. The pickup is a DeArmond "floating" type.

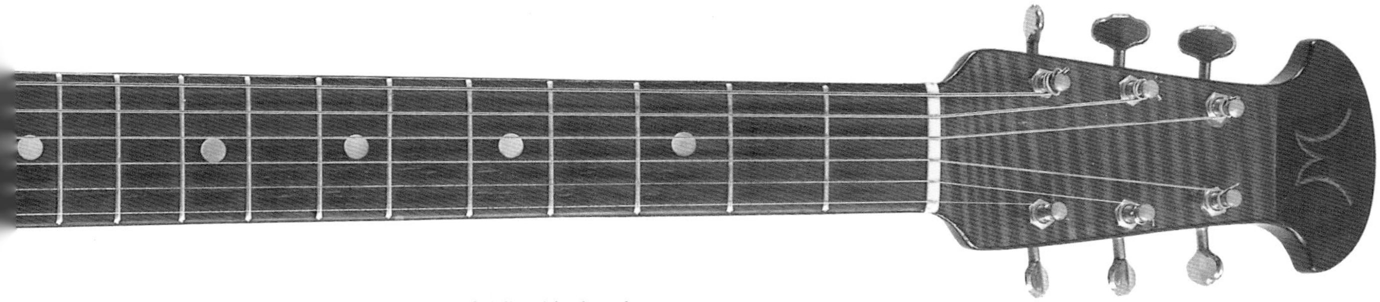

▼ GIBSON ES-300

PRODUCED: *1940-1942 (this style)*

THIS EXAMPLE: *1941; serial 96762*

BODY: *16½" wide, 3¼" deep*

At first the ES-300 had a bigger slant-mounted pickup, but soon settled on the type shown here. Guitar production ceased at Gibson when the war came in 1942, and few pre-war pickup styles survived. The 300 was the first Gibson to feature the "crown" headstock inlay, widely used elsewhere since then.

▲ WILKANOWSKI AIRWAY W2

PRODUCED: *c1939-1940*

THIS EXAMPLE: *c1939; serial 1*

BODY: *16" wide, 3⅜" deep*

Wilkanowski was a violin maker who emigrated to the United States from Poland, probably around 1920, at first working in Boston and later in New York. He is thought to have made in the region of 30 guitars. Compared to his much greater output of violins, it's clear that to describe his guitars even as a sideline would be something of an exaggeration. Quite why he made the few guitars he did is unknown, although an unsupported story suggests that a friend whose son wanted a guitar asked Wilkanowski to make him an instrument. From the little information that has become available, it seems that Wilkanowski did not make any more guitars beyond about 1941.

▲ GIBSON L-5 PREMIERE

PRODUCED: *1939-1983 (also L-5C)*

THIS EXAMPLE: *1940; serial 96617*

BODY: *16½" wide, 3½" deep*

Gibson offered the Super 400 and the L-5 models with its new Premiere cutaway body from 1939. "Quickly and easily, without the slightest extra effort, you can reach all 20 frets in this new body design," said the company's 1940 catalog, showing Eddie Skrivanek with the cutaway L-5. "It gives you more notes, more chords, greater variety, and much greater playing comfort."

the case for Wilkanowski violins) but no more guitars are dated beyond these examples from around 1939 and 1940.

Meanwhile, and of course with much more contemporary documentation to help the modern guitar historian, a number of developments were occurring at the Gibson company's factory over in Kalamazoo, Michigan. The cutaway-type Premiere body option that had successfully been applied during 1939 to the leading archtop in the Gibson line, the Super 400, was also offered on the company's other great f-hole guitar of the period, the L-5. Gibson was also building on its experiments earlier in the 1930s with electric instruments, when guitars such as the low-end ES-150 were offered, and in 1940 the company introduced its most expensive pre-war electric model, the ES-300.

1947

LEO FENDER RENAMES HIS
BUSINESS THE FENDER
ELECTRIC INSTRUMENT CO.

*From humble beginnings in
California in the mid-1940s,
Fender was to become one of the
most radical guitar makers of the
1950s and 1960s, shaking up the
industry with boldly styled, mass
produced solidbody electric
guitars that changed forever the
way in which guitars were
produced and marketed.*

▼ **FENDER TELECASTER**

PRODUCED: *1951-current*

THIS EXAMPLE: *c1964; serial L25028*

BODY: *12¼" wide, 1⅜" deep*

*This Telecaster has been fitted with a
Parsons-White B-Bender. Invented by
Byrds guitarist Clarence White and*
*drummer/banjoist Gene Parsons, it
has a series of internal levers (see
back, left) that connect the strap
button to the bridge. When the
player "pulls" on the guitar strap the
levers move the bridge and raise the
pitch of the B-string, giving bends
within chords to emulate pedal
steel type sounds.*

Leo Fender's earliest production guitars were lap steel types,
made at first in the mid-1940s with his partner Doc Kauffman
under the K&F brand, but soon after as Fender guitars, along
with a complimentary line of small amplifiers.

Working in Fullerton, in Orange County, California, and
barely surviving difficult financial times, Leo Fender gradually
began to consider the possibility of a new type of instrument,
a solidbody electric Spanish guitar. There were few
precedents. An Orange County engineer, Paul
Bigsby (see p.82), made a solidbody electric guitar
for country musician Merle Travis in the late 1940s,
and it seems certain that Leo did in fact see and
probably examined that instrument. Another firm
based in California, Rickenbacker, had produced a semi-

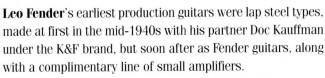

solid Bakelite electric guitar as long ago as 1935 (see p.68),
but that had been something of a commercial failure.

Fender wanted to make a solidbody not for musical
reasons, but because it would be easier to produce.
The company's first solidbody guitars were the Esquire and
Broadcaster of 1950, the latter soon renamed the Telecaster
and today the longest-running solidbody electric guitar in
production. As Tony Bacon and Paul Day put it in
The Fender Book: "Fender made the electric guitar
into a factory product, stripped down to its essential
elements, built up from easily assembled parts, and
produced at an affordable price. Fender's methods
made for easier, more consistent production – and
a different sound. Not for Fender the fat, Gibson-style

▼ FENDER STRATOCASTER

PRODUCED: *1954-current*

THIS EXAMPLE: *1959; serial 34690*

BODY: *12¼" wide, 1" deep*

Strats with a blonde finish and gold-plated hardware were first issued early in 1957, Fender's first official custom color guitars. They have

become known among collectors as "Mary Kaye" Strats for a musician who appeared with such a guitar in Fender catalogs at the time. To many, the Mary Kaye is the epitome of the Stratocaster, so beautiful and elegant. The combination of the body color and the gold hardware works so well, and the instrument really comes together perfectly.

▲ FENDER STRATOCASTER

PRODUCED: *1954-current*

THIS EXAMPLE: *1964; serial L59710*

BODY: *12¼" wide, 1" deep*

In 1959 the Strat changed from maple to a glued-on rosewood fingerboard. The maple playing surface became stained after it had been played a number of times, but rosewood kept its looks. Fender had first made the material change with the introduction of its new Jazzmaster model in '59 – and for a spectacular display of Jazzmasters please turn to the colorful selection illustrated over pages 99 to 101.

▲ FENDER STRATOCASTER

PRODUCED: *1954-current*

THIS EXAMPLE: *Dec. 1956; serial 09286*

BODY: *12¼" wide, 1" deep*

Here's a fine, original example of the earliest style of Stratocaster. This first-period Strat has the distinctive

features of the period, including frets set directly into the face of the bolt-on maple neck, a round string retainer and "spaghetti" Fender logo on the small peghead, and a single-ply white pickguard with eight mounting screws on a body finished in clear nitro-cellulose lacquer over a two-tone sunburst effect.

▶ FENDER MANDOLIN

PRODUCED: *1956-1976*

THIS EXAMPLE: *c1960; serial 02343*

BODY: *10" wide, 1½" deep*

Fender's four-string electric mandolin was designed in the mid-1950s, aimed at Western swing players who doubled on mandolin.

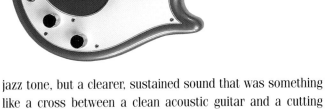

The look and style of Fender literature was almost as eye catching as the guitars themselves; even a logo for a string packet (above) had the elegant simplicity that ran through the entire product line.

jazz tone, but a clearer, sustained sound that was something like a cross between a clean acoustic guitar and a cutting electric lap steel."

Fender's masterstroke came just a few years later with the Stratocaster, a stylish three-pickup solidbody that went on to become an industry standard, and which would fire the music of players as diverse as Buddy Holly and Jimi Hendrix. When it was launched in 1954, the Stratocaster looked like no other guitar around. In time it would become one of the most popular and most desired electric guitars ever made.

▼ FENDER DUO-SONIC CUSTOM

PRODUCED: *1956-1964 (this style)*

THIS EXAMPLE: *1961; serial 61475*

BODY: *10¾" wide, 1½" deep*

The Duo-Sonic model was one of Fender's first short-scale "student" guitars. It seems that this

Duo-Sonic with a clear plastic body may have been an experimental prototype for a model that Fender considered producing, or for display at instrument trade shows as a means of drawing attention to the company's exhibit. Reports suggest that there was also a Stratocaster with a clear plastic body made around the same time as this guitar.

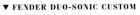

1949

*GIBSON INTRODUCES THE
FIRST THREE-PICKUP GUITAR*

*Gibson upstages the growing
number of competitors who are
joining the electric guitar industry
by launching the very first
instrument to be fitted with three
pickups. Where other makers are
content with the traditional
compliment of one or two
pickups, Gibson feels that its new
ES-5 will lead the market in
electronic munificence.*

▲ GIBSON ES-350 SPECIAL

THIS EXAMPLE: *Jul. 1949: serial A3372*

BODY: *17" wide, 3⅜" deep*

*This is a rare prototype version of
the ES-5, masquerading as a three-
pickup ES-350. The guitar is one of
an experimental batch of 12 such*
*guitars made by Gibson during June
and July 1949. The company's
record for this guitar, entered into
the factory logbook at the time, has
a handwritten "ES-350 Sp." (for
"Special") over which has been
stamped in ink "ES-5." Clearly what
we have here is the birth of Gibson's
ES-5 guitar, in its earliest form.*

Gibson's archtop f-hole electric guitar had come on in leaps
and bounds since the company's earliest experiments in the
1930s with models such as the ground-breaking ES-150.
Soon the budget ES-100 and high-end ES-300 were added,
before America's entry into World War II in 1942 when Gibson
effectively put a halt to its guitar production. As instrument
manufacturing recommenced after the war, Gibson rightly
believed that the electric guitar was set to become an
important part of its reactivated business.

The significant new archtop electrics that debuted during
this period – the ES-350 of 1947, and the ES-175 and ES-5 of
1949 – were aimed at players who were prepared to commit
themselves to fully electric instruments that were designed
and built as such by Gibson. It was also at this time that

Gibson began to pioneer electric guitars with cutaways. This
made a good deal of sense. In some musical settings there
was little point in playing high up the neck of acoustic guitars
as the results might not be audible. But on an instrument
equipped with a pickup and suitably amplified, a cutaway
offered easier access to the now audible and musically useful
area of the upper fingerboard. Talented and imaginative
players openly welcomed the artistic potential of the cutaway
and began to investigate the dusty end of the fingerboard.

The ES-350 of 1947 was the first of the new style cutaway
Gibson electrics (and indeed at first it bore the "Premier" tag of
the pre-war cutaway acoustics). The ES-350 was followed in
1949 by the new ES-175, Gibson's first electric with a "pointed"
cutaway style and a pressed, laminated top. The ES-5

◄ **GIBSON ES-5 SWITCHMASTER**

PRODUCED: *1956-1961*

THIS EXAMPLE: *Apr. 1957; serial 25374*

BODY: *16¾" wide, 3⅜" deep*

Guitarist Jimmy Pruett, original owner of this guitar, added a customized pickguard to what is a fine, early ES-5 Switchmaster. This example has the original P-90 single-coil pickups that were used on the Switchmaster from its launch in 1956 until 1958. In that year the company's new humbucking pickups were employed on most of the

electric lines, and the elegant loop-design tailpiece was a fixture of all but the very earliest examples of the Switchmaster. By 1961 the model's "rounded" cutaway had given way to the "pointed" style cutaway that Gibson applied to most of its electrics at that time. During its life, the ES-5 Switchmaster was never an especially popular guitar. According to factory records, Gibson made a total of 334 sunburst ES-5s (including seven samples in 1955). As usual, natural finish versions were made in smaller numbers; just 167 natural ES-5s were shipped.

appeared in the same year as the 175, and was among the earliest (and indeed probably the very first) electric guitars to be offered with a compliment of three pickups.

A 1950 catalog described the new ES-5 in glowing terms: "The supreme electronic version of the famed Gibson L-5, the ES-5 Electric Spanish Guitar combines the acclaimed features of the L-5 with the finest method of electronic guitar

▶ **GIBSON SUPER 400CES**

PRODUCED: *1951-current*

THIS EXAMPLE: *Jun. 1960; serial A33851*

BODY: *18" wide, 3⅜" deep*

*Gibson's finest electric archtop
guitar, the Super 400CES, was
built with the best materials.
The body is made with a
carved spruce top (which,
Gibson explained in catalogs
of the time, was "unusual for
an electric guitar"), while
maple is used for the back,
sides and neck, and ebony
for the fingerboard. The
CES models of 1951 – the
L-5CES and the Super
400CES – were the first
Gibson electrics to use a
control layout that had a
volume and tone for each
pickup, a scheme that was
quickly adopted for most of
the company's electric models.*

In 1954 Gibson's historian Julius Bellson charted the 16-year
progress of the company's electric guitars. Consulting
records, Bellson estimated that back in 1938 electric guitars
had made up no more than ten per cent of Gibson guitar
sales, but that the proportion of electrics to the rest had risen
to 15 per cent by 1940, to 50 per cent by 1951, and that by
1953 electric guitars constituted no less than 65 per cent of
the Kalamazoo, Michigan, company's total guitar sales.

Gibson had toyed with what it described as an electric
version of its fine L-5 acoustic archtop in 1949, the three-
pickup ES-5 (see p.74), but this always seemed more like an
expanded ES-350. Still keen on the general idea, in 1951
Gibson decided to get serious about the electric guitar, and
launched two excellent new guitars based on its most
prestigious archtop models,
the Super 400 and the L-5. The
company's L-5 guitar provided the basis for the year's first
new electric, the L-5CES (the initials stand for Cutaway,
Electric, Spanish), while the Super 400 in electric guise
became the new top-of-the-line electric archtop for Gibson,
the Super 400CES. In the case of this guitar, Gibson took its
existing Super 400C acoustic model and provided it with two
P90 pickups and associated controls, as well as modified,

▲ **GIBSON SUPER 400CES**

PRODUCED: *1951-current*

THIS EXAMPLE: *Feb 1953; serial A12848*

BODY: *18" wide, 3⅜" deep*

*Here is a Super 400CES in sunburst
with P90 pickups. During the
instrument's first ten years – the
"rounded cutaway" period of 1951 to
1960 – Gibson made only 108 natural
examples and 152 sunbursts.*

1951

GIBSON INTRODUCES ITS
NEW CES ELECTRICS

*The Super 400CES and the
L-5CES are introduced at the top
of Gibson's pricelist, underlining
the company's serious attitude to
electric archtop guitars and
providing a new challenge to
other makers.*

▲ GIBSON SUPER 400CES

PRODUCED: *1951-current*

THIS EXAMPLE: *May 1958; serial A27558*

BODY: *18" wide, 3⅜" deep*

*This guitar illustrates that Super
400s were still leaving the factory in
1958 with Alnico pickups, whereas
some Gibson electrics had been
fitted with humbuckers since 1957.*

▲ GIBSON SUPER 400CESN

PRODUCED: *1951-current*

THIS EXAMPLE: *Jul. 1952; serial A11223*

BODY: *18" wide, 3⅜" deep*

*Gibson had made some earlier
experimental attempts at producing
an electric version of the Super 400,*
*including an interesting 1939 test
that can be seen on p.65. Howev[er]
wasn't until 1951 that the
company's official CES version
appeared. (Some of the earliest
examples are labeled "SEC" inste[ad]
of "CES.") The beautiful natural
finish model shown here comes f[rom]
the second year of production.*

▼ VEGA 1200 STEREO

PRODUCED: *1959*

THIS EXAMPLE: *1959; serial 10750*

BODY: *16½″ wide, 3½″ deep*

Vega not only made normal guitars like the E-300 (left) at this time, but experimented with designs such as

this bizarre 12-pickup stereo instrument, made in the same year as Gibson's stereo guitars (see p.104). The Vega's pickups are split into two groups of six, two for each string – the rear six are for treble, the front six for bass – and were designed to feed a pair of amplifiers for an on-stage stereo effect.

▲ VEGA E-300 DUO-TRON

PRODUCED: *1949-1956*

THIS EXAMPLE: *1951; serial 7754*

BODY: *16⅛″ wide, 3½″ deep*

Meanwhile in Boston, Vega's E-300 had a pickup and controls that "floated" above the body to retain an acoustic tone in an electric guitar.

◄ GIBSON ES-175N

PRODUCED: *1949-1971*

THIS EXAMPLE: *Jun. 1956; serial A2335*

BODY: *15¾″ wide, 3½″ deep*

The small-body 175 added a distinctive tone color to Gibson's electric line, its pressed, laminated maple/basswood body contributing to a bright and cutting sound. An optional two-pickup version, the 175D, was added to the line in 1953.

---

plification. Three separately controlled, adjustable, gnetic pickups reproduce the full, rich tones and monics to make the ES-5 truly 'the instrument of a usand voices.'" Despite Gibson's assertion, and as sically demonstrated by the rare ES-350 shown here (far , the ES-5 was actually more like a three-pickup ES-350. efore long, it became apparent that the original ES-5 was as controllable as many players might like. As with all son's immediate post-war electric guitars, the ES-5 had no up switching. Instead, each pickup had a separate volume rol (there was also an overall tone knob). Setting the e volume knobs at relative positions was the only way to eve a balance between the pickups' sounds. And so in 6 Gibson issued the ES-5 with redesigned electronics, as

the ES-5 Switchmaster. Gibson said that this new model brought to the guitarist "an increased range of performance." Three individual tone knobs were added to the three volume controls, and a four-way pickup selector switch (hence the Switchmaster name) was added near the cutaway. The switch, explained a Gibson catalog of the time, "activates each of the three pickups separately, a combination of any two, or all three simultaneously." At a time when Fender had just launched its stylish three-pickup Stratocaster, and Epiphone was offering models with a six-button "color tone" switching system, Gibson probably felt the ES-5 Switchmaster was a potential market leader. But it never caught on. And anyway, in 1951 Gibson had produced proper electric versions of both the L-5 and the Super 400.

▲ GIBSON ES-5

PRODUCED: *1949-1956*

THIS EXAMPLE: *Nov. 1950; serial A6251*

BODY: *16¾″ wide, 3½″ deep*

Here is an outstandingly beautiful example of the sunburst ES-5, in the model's original guise before it received the Switchmaster redesign during 1956 (see far left, above). Between the model's launch in 1949 and the change in 1956, Gibson shipped a total of 908 ES-5 models, of which 577 were, like this second-year example, finished in sunburst, and just 331 in natural.

◄ GIBSON SUPER 400CESN

PRODUCED: 1951-current

THIS EXAMPLE: Dec 1958; serial A28868

BODY: 18" wide, 3⅜" deep

By the end of 1958 Gibson's new humbucking pickups had arrived on the Super 400CES, as demonstrated by this attractive natural finish example. Until 1962, Gibson's humbuckers had small "Patent Applied For" labels fixed to their base, and these "PAF" versions are now generally considered to be among the best sounding pickups that Gibson have ever produced.

▲ GIBSON SUPER 400CES SPECIAL

THIS EXAMPLE: Dec 1953; serial A15987

BODY: 18" wide, 33/8" deep

Most of the Gibson Super 400CES guitars on these pages started as part of the collection assembled by Thomas A. Van Hoose (acoustics start on p.64) which was then built upon by Scott Chinery. One such addition was this incredible seven-string Super 400CES. It was custom built at the end of 1953 by Gibson, and company ledgers reveal that this unusual guitar – it has no fewer than three P90 pickups that feed a separate tripod-mounted control box (not shown) – was specially ordered for an inspired customer of Sherman Clay, a California musical instrument store.

stronger internal bracing so that it would be less prone to feedback when amplified. The generally large proportions of the 18-inch wide body were retained for this most impressive of Gibson's electric archtops, as were the acoustic 400's upscale appointments such as split-block fingerboard inlays, "marbleized" tortoiseshell pickguard and a split-diamond headstock inlay. On these three pages we show the Super 400CES in its first "rounded cutaway" style. This lasted from the model's launch in 1951 until 1960, when a new "pointed cutaway" style of body was introduced by Gibson (some examples of this later type can be seen overleaf).

Gibson made some changes to the pickups of the Super 400CES during the 1950s, and these changes are also documented here. At first the electric 400 came with a pair of Gibson's standard single-coil P90 pickups, but in 1954 these were changed to "Alnico" types with distinctive rectangular polepieces. The Alnico nickname comes from the magnet type used in the pickups. During 1957 Gibson started to fit its electric guitars with new humbucking pickups, developed by Seth Lover in the Gibson labs, and the Super 400CES soon began to appear with these new units.

An immense variety of players has at different times been drawn to the power and versatility of the Super 400CES, including bluesman Robben Ford, country players like Hank Thompson and Merle Travis (whose custom 400 was in 1952 Gibson's "most expensive guitar ever"), rock'n'roller Scotty Moore with Elvis Presley, and a number of fine jazz guitarists such as George Benson and Kenny Burrell.

▲ **GIBSON SUPER 400CES**

PRODUCED: *1951-current*

THIS EXAMPLE: *Jun. 1969; serial 567108*

BODY: *18″ wide, 3⅜″ deep*

Gibson's change of cutaway styles on the Super 400CES almost splits the model into convenient decades of production. The first "rounded"

cutaway style was made between 1951 and 1960, the second "pointed" type between 1960 and 1969, and the final rounded cutaway version, like this sunburst example, was made from early 1969 onwards. Note also the very attractive back of this guitar (above), showing the fine woods that Gibson selected for the Super 400CES at the time.

▼ GIBSON SUPER 400CESN

PRODUCED: *1951-current*

THIS EXAMPLE: *Nov. 1962; serial 61315*

BODY: *18" wide, 3½" deep*

Gibson's "sharp" cutaway was introduced to the Super 400CES in 1960, and offered much deeper access into the very highest frets on the fingerboard. Gibson's records indicate that between 1960 and 1968 it produced 272 sunburst 400CESs and 103 natural versions.

► GIBSON SUPER 400CES

PRODUCED: *1951-current*

THIS EXAMPLE: *Jun. 1964; serial 64660*

BODY: *18" wide, 3½" deep*

Elvis Presley's guitarist Scotty Moore was a convert to the new "pointed" Super 400CES, and a similar guitar to this sunburst example had its most famous exposure in both Moore's and Presley's hands on Elvis's comeback TV show, broadcast by NBC in December 1968.

▼ GIBSON SUPER 400CES-WR

PRODUCED: *1976-1980*

THIS EXAMPLE: *Nov. 1977; serial 73367124*

BODY: *18" wide, 3⅜" deep*

Usually available only in sunburst or natural finishes, in the late 1970s

the 400CES was offered in two further color options: the wine red of the example shown here, and ebony. These were apparently introduced to use up stocks of plainer wood that were less suitable for natural or sunburst guitars, where lack of grain or figure would be more obvious.

The Super 400CES changed to a "sharp" cutaway during 1960. The earlier "rounded" style (see p.77) is generally referred to by Gibson as the Venetian cutaway, while the newer "pointed" type is officially called the Florentine cutaway. The origin of these terms is not clear.

In fact this new cutaway design, first used on the ES-175 that had been introduced back in 1949, was in many ways more difficult to manufacture than the older style. Where the "rounded" style used one continuous piece of wood for the side, or "rim," bent to the curved contour of the cutaway, the new "sharp" cutaway required two pieces of wood for this section. One piece went from the side of the neck to the "point," and then another piece continued around the rest of that side of the guitar. The design also needed a deeper

mahogany neck block than the earlier type because of the depth of the new cutaway. No doubt these changes took extra time and effort at the Gibson factory in Kalamazoo.

Gibson enticed players to the new style with the assurance that it was "a modern, deep cutaway design," and "provides easy access to the entire fret range." However, probably due to cost considerations caused by the extra work involved with the new design, Gibson reverted to the original "rounded" cutaway style for the Super 400CES early in 1969.

Thomas A. Van Hoose sums up the appeal of the Super 400CES in his *Gibson Super 400* book: "When plugged in, the Super 400CES really came into its own, producing a deep tone with much color that was in sharp contrast to other electric guitars available up to that time."

▲ SUPER 400CES 50th ANNIVERSARY

PRODUCED: *1984*

THIS EXAMPLE: *Apr. 1984; serial 81104003*

BODY: *18" wide, 3⅜" deep*

Gibson closed its Kalamazoo factory in 1984, moving production to Nashville. Coincidentally, 1984 was 50 years from the introduction of the Super 400 model. So around ten Super 400CES guitars, the last to come from Kalamazoo, were marked "50th Anniversary" at the 19th fret. The final production at Kalamazoo was in June 1984, after more than 65 years' worthy service for Gibson.

1952

BIGSBY MAKES FIRST ELECTRIC DOUBLE-NECK

A true innovator in solidbody guitars, Paul A. Bigsby builds a custom electric guitar for country musician Grady Martin that has guitar and five-string mandolin necks in one instrument.

▲ **GIBSON EDS-1275 DOUBLE 12**

PRODUCED: *1958-1962 (this style)*

THIS EXAMPLE: *1960; serial 010523*

BODY: *17" wide, 2" deep*

Gibson began making electric double-necks six years after Bigsby's first effort. In 1962 Gibson's double-necks moved to a solidbody style.

▼ **BIGSBY MANDOLIN**

THIS EXAMPLE: *May 1950; serial 51550*

BODY: *10¾" wide, 2" deep*

As well as vibrato systems, steel guitars, Spanish guitars and double-necks, Bigsby also made solid mandolins. Mandolin market leader Gibson produced its own solidbody mandolin, the Florentine, four years after this Bigsby appeared.

▶ GIBSON EMS-1235 DOUBLE MANDOLIN

PRODUCED: *1961-1962 (this style)*

THIS EXAMPLE: *Sep. 1962; serial 17714*

BODY: *17" wide, 2¼" deep*

Despite the "Double Mandolin" name, the shorter neck of this Gibson model was in fact a short-scale six-string neck that was designed to be tuned an octave higher than the regular neck. Gibson's double-neck guitars were advertised as available only to special order, and from the scarcity of examples today it seems that few were produced.

◀ BIGSBY DOUBLE-NECK

THIS EXAMPLE: *Oct. 1952; serial 10152*

BODY: *14" wide, 2" deep*

Grady Martin was one of the busiest session guitarists on the Nashville scene, where he started on fiddle in the 1940s. Especially notable was his work with Marty Robbins and Patsy Cline. This astonishing double-neck, the first electric instrument of its kind, was specially built for Martin by Paul Bigsby. Martin

recalls: "I designed this guitar from a piece of cardboard, and played it in the 1950s and 1960s on hundreds of early Nashville recordings as well as some in L.A.

and New York. It was my only electric guitar at that time." Martin is pictured with the guitar on the 1954 Slew Foot Five sleeve (left). It's interesting to note the Stratocaster-like peghead shape and three guitar pickups, some two years before the Fender. There's a master tone knob by the cutaway, a single white knob to control the mandolin pickup, and the black knobs are for the guitar's pickups. The switch selects between mandolin, "standby" mode and guitar. Typical Bigsby solidbody features include the birdseye figured maple and aluminum pickup covers.

▼ CARVIN 2-MS DOUBLE-NECK

PRODUCED: *1959-c1970*

THIS EXAMPLE: *c1965*

BODY: *12⅜" wide, 1⅝" deep*

Carvin was started by Lowell Kiesel in California in the mid-1940s, and was soon selling guitars and other gear by mail order. This unusual guitar and mandolin double-neck was part of a line of Carvin solidbody instruments launched in the 1950s. Carvin is still in business today.

Paul A. Bigsby worked in Downey, California, as a pattern-maker, engineer and mechanic. Bigsby was also a keen motorcyclist who loved to tinker with machines, and came into contact with local musicians who valued his mechanical skills. Bigsby remains well known among players for his vibrato system, one of the earliest on the market. In 1948 Bigsby built a solidbody guitar for country guitarist and songwriter Merle Travis.

This turned out to be a very significant instrument historically. It was closer to the modern idea of a solid electric guitar than anything that had been made before, and it certainly influenced Leo Fender's commercially successful solidbody electric guitars that would appear in the early 1950s (see p.72). Travis wrote in 1980 that he had gone to

Bigsby with the idea of a guitar that would have a body "thin and solid. That way it'll keep ringing like a steel." Bigsby had made steel guitars for players such as Speedy West in the late 1940s, and he built the solid Spanish electric to Travis's design in a similar fashion: the neck was one piece from peghead to body tip (now known as "through-neck" style).

Another historically significant instrument from among Bigsby's small output was the double-neck shown here, specially built for another country guitarist, Grady Martin. The idea behind a double-neck is that a musician can use one guitar to provide an instant changeover between two entirely different instruments. Despite the disadvantage of weight and relative awkwardness, further double-neck electric guitars appeared over the years following Bigsby's innovation.

1952

GIBSON LAUNCHES ITS FIRST
SOLIDBODY ELECTRIC

*Hard on the heels of the new
Fender solidbody, Gibson signs up
Les Paul, the most famous
guitarist of the day, to help sell its
own version of the solidbody
phenomenon. The company's Les
Paul Model contrasts a striking
gold finish designed for
commercial appeal with a carved-
top body that underlines Gibson's
craft heritage.*

◄ **GIBSON LES PAUL JUMBO**

PRODUCED: *1970-1971*

THIS EXAMPLE: *c1970; serial 902402*

BODY: *15¾" wide, 4¾" deep*

*One of the more unusual (and rare)
members of the family of Gibson Les
Paul guitars was the flat-top Jumbo.
Its low impedance pickup is of a type
that Gibson fitted to a number of
new Les Paul models around 1970.*

▲ **GIBSON LES PAUL "CHERRY RED"**

PRODUCED: *c1958-1959*

THIS EXAMPLE: *1959; serial 9 3017*

BODY: *12¾" wide, 2" deep*

*Gibson had first applied the new
cherry red color to its Les Paul
Junior model in 1958. During that*

*year and the next the company
made a very small number of regular
Les Pauls with a cherry red finish,
and original examples are extremely
rare today. The color was also used
by Gibson for the revamped Les Paul
Special and the ES-355 of 1959,
and was offered as an option on the
ES-335 model from 1960.*

▲ **GIBSON LES PAUL "GOLD-TOP"**

PRODUCED: *1952-current*

THIS EXAMPLE: *1952*

BODY: *12¾" wide, 2" deep*

*Gibson described its new solidbody
electric Les Paul Model as a "unique
and exciting innovation in the fretted
instrument field," and at first other
makers were surprised that the*

*conservative Gibson company should
indulge in the new solidbody style,
seen by some as a kind of second
class guitar. Gibson called it the Les
Paul Model; today it is known as the
"gold-top" thanks to the arresting
paint finish. This is an especially
early example, and the non-standard
black pickups (they are white on
production versions) imply that it
could have been a prototype.*

▲ **GIBSON LES PAUL "GOLD-TOP"**

PRODUCED: *1952-current*

THIS EXAMPLE: *1957; serial 7 6981*

BODY: *12¾" wide, 2" deep*

In 1955 Gibson added its new Tune-o-Matic bridge, as on this example, and humbucking pickups came in 1957. The result was a combination of features that many consider add up to one of the finest solidbody guitars of all time. Desirable enough in this gold-top form, the sunburst Les Paul of 1958-1960 (see p.86) is now a blue chip vintage instrument.

▲ **GIBSON LES PAUL CUSTOM**

PRODUCED: *1957-1961 (this style)*

THIS EXAMPLE: *1957; serial 7 8512*

BODY: *12¾" wide, 2" deep*

The Custom appeared in revised form in 1957 when the original two-pickup layout (see below) was replaced with three of the company's new humbucking pickups. This was probably a reaction to Fender's three-pickup Stratocaster of 1954 that was gaining in popularity.

Les Paul started his professional life as a teenage guitarist during the 1930s broadcasting on radio stations, playing country as "Rhubarb Red" and dipping into R&B and jazz as well. Around 1940 he had toyed with his own ideas of how an electric guitar should be put together, modifying his hollow body Epiphone guitar to make what he called the "log." Paul inserted a central four-by-four block of solid pine between the cut halves of the Epi's dismembered body, and added a couple of crude homemade pickups for good measure.

Les Paul modified two more Epiphones – this time naming them "clunkers" – and would choose between the adapted Epiphones for stage and studio work throughout the 1940s and into the early 1950s. Paul says that around 1946 he took his "log" to Gibson to see if they would like to produce such a

guitar, but was laughed out of the building. Over the next few years, Les Paul became famous. He played on a Bing Crosby hit, and then was signed himself to Capitol Records. His first release, 'Lover,' which used the overdubbing techniques he'd developed, got to 21 on the chart in 1948.

But it was when he teamed up with singer/guitarist Mary Ford (they married in 1949) that the big hits started, especially 'How High The Moon,' a #1 smash in 1951. Gibson, meanwhile, was keeping its eye on the upstart Leo Fender whose solidbody guitars were gaining in popularity. Deciding to make a Gibson solidbody, company boss Ted McCarty called in Les Paul. A deal was struck for the famous guitarist to endorse the company's new solidbody electric, launched in 1952. The Gibson Les Paul Model was born.

▲ **GIBSON LES PAUL CUSTOM**

PRODUCED: *1954-1957 (this style)*

THIS EXAMPLE: *c1954*

BODY: *12¾" wide, 2" deep*

Following the gold-top Les Paul came the Custom, introduced in 1954. It was a sleek, high-end instrument, finished in black and with gold-plated hardware. This example has non-standard pickups, probably a trial design or early prototype. Gibson used a P90 and "Alnico" on the production Custom.

▼ GIBSON LES PAUL "SUNBURST"

PRODUCED: *1958-1960, 1985-current*

THIS EXAMPLE: *1960; serial 0 0608*

BODY: *12¾" wide, 2" deep*

For many players, the choice is still between a Les Paul or a Strat for the prime solidbody electric. The phenomenon of old Les Pauls among connoisseurs, is that there's a soul to these instruments, a quality that seems to transcend modern examples, despite increasingly impressive re-creations. The three sunburst Les Pauls here show some of the variations that exist in the "flame" or figure of the maple tops.

Sales of Gibson's Les Paul gold-top gradually declined during the late 1950s, and in 1958 Gibson changed its look by applying a more traditional cherry sunburst finish. The company must have calculated that the unusual gold finish of the original instrument was too unconventional. And to some extent they were proved right. Sales of the gold-top had declined from a high of 920 in 1956 to just 434 in 1958, the year of the new sunburst finish. Sales then climbed to 643 in 1959, but when they dipped again in 1960 Gibson decided that the only way to attract new customers was completely to redesign the Les Paul. So the sunburst model was dropped, having existed for a little short of three years.

But the shortlived sunburst made a comeback. During the middle and late 1960s a number of guitarists discovered that the instrument had enormous potential for high volume blues-based rock. Leading early members of the Les Paul appreciation society were Mike Bloomfield in the U.S. and Eric Clapton in the U.K. – Bloomfield with the Butterfield Blues Band, and Clapton with John Mayall's Bluesbreakers. Demand for Les Pauls rocketed, Gibson reintroduced the early design in 1968, and in the following years the original sunburst Les Pauls achieved almost mythological status. Players and collectors realized that the guitar's short production run and inherent musicality added up to a modern classic. Today, the 1958-1960 sunburst Les Paul "Standard" is among the most valuable of all guitars.

▼ GIBSON BYRDLAND SPECIAL

THIS EXAMPLE: *c1967; serial 849728*

BODY: *16¾" wide, 2¼" deep*

This unusual custom-made Gibson has the general features of the Byrdland model of 1955 – shorter, narrower neck,

fancy tailpiece, block fingerboard markers and "flower pot" peghead inlay – but with the double-cutaway full-depth body of the Barney Kessel model that had been introduced in 1961. The odd combination was ordered by original owner Willie Luedecke, whose name appears in place of "Byrdland" on the tailpiece.

▲ GIBSON ES-295

PRODUCED: *1952-1958*

THIS EXAMPLE: *May 1957; serial A25611*

BODY: *15¾" wide, 3½" deep*

At the same time as the Les Paul gold-top, Gibson also introduced this gold hollow electric. At first it came

with Gibson's P90 pickups, but in 1957 humbuckers were fitted. The model lasted just another year, so this is a relatively rare variation. A total of 1,770 ES-295s were shipped in the model's seven-year life, but only 120 during 1957 and 1958 (including some in 1957 that would still have been fitted with P90s).

▼ GIBSON LES PAUL "SUNBURST"

PRODUCED: *1958-1960, 1985-current*

THIS EXAMPLE: *1993; serial 9 0012*

BODY: *12¾" wide, 2" deep*

Ever aware of the growing value of its old guitars on the vintage market, Gibson began in 1985

to make a reissue based on the famous Les Paul sunburst of 1959. At first called the "59 Re-issue," the model in 1993 became the "59 Les Paul Flametop," part of Gibson's Historic Collection. This 59 Reissue is the actual guitar used to advertise the Historic Collection Les Pauls, as seen in the poster below.

▲ GIBSON LES PAUL "SUNBURST"

PRODUCED: *1958-1960, 1985-current*

THIS EXAMPLE: *1960; serial 0 8160*

BODY: *12¾" wide, 2" deep*

"If it ain't got wood it ain't no good" is how collectors of the Les Paul 'burst sum up their addiction to a visually striking pattern, or "figure," in the guitar's maple top.

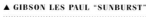

THE HISTORIC COLLECTION

▲ GIBSON LES PAUL "SUNBURST"

PRODUCED: *1958-1960, 1985-current*

THIS EXAMPLE: *1960; serial 010838*

BODY: *12¾" wide, 2" deep*

The maple "cap" of the Les Paul gold-top was hidden under its solid paint finish, but the new sunburst

model had a semi-transparent finish that showed off the underlying wood. So Gibson would "bookmatch" the maple to give symmetrically appealing patterns. The company's most impressive maple was reserved for archtop backs, but some Les Paul sunbursts, like those here, are very attractive; others are quite plain.

Gibson's Historic Collection, launched in 1993, consists of a number of "replicas" of old guitars, including a 59 Les Paul Flametop and 60 Les Paul Flametop. This poster shows the actual Les Paul pictured above, and was signed by various Gibson personnel to authenticate the instrument.

1953

MACCAFERRI INTRODUCES
PLASTIC GUITARS

Continuing from a riotously successful plastic ukulele, and exploiting the relatively new technology of injection molded plastics, Italian immigrant Mario Maccaferri launches a line of plastic guitars that, despite high quality and low prices, fails to impress the conservative guitarists of the day.

◄ **MACCAFERRI G-40**

PRODUCED: *1953-c1958*

THIS EXAMPLE: *c1955*

BODY: *13¼" wide, 3½" deep*

Maccaferri's first plastic guitars were the flat-top G-30 ($29.95) and archtop G-40 ($39.95) of 1953, manufactured by his French American Reed company in New York. The neck was bolted to the body, and despite a plastic exterior had a central metal core that extended the length of the instrument: the "stay true neck" of Maccaferri's ads, which also boasted that the plastic guitars were "not affected by atmospheric conditions – will not crack or swell."

◄ **SELMER MACCAFERRI JAZZ**

PRODUCED: *France, 1932-c1935 (this style)*

THIS EXAMPLE: *1932; serial 103*

BODY: *15½" wide, 3⅞" deep*

Django Reinhardt used a number of Selmer Maccaferri-style guitars in his career, including at first a D-hole model like this, and later oval-hole guitars (below). Researcher François Charle estimates no more than 100 of this D-hole Jazz model were built.

▶ **SELMER JAZZ**

PRODUCED: *France, c1934-1952 (this style)*

THIS EXAMPLE: *1951; serial 848*

BODY: *15½" wide, 3⅝" deep*

After Maccaferri left Selmer the company continued to make guitars of similar design but with a modified oval soundhole. This is one of the last hundred made of a total of around 500 in this style. Altogether, in the 20 years from 1932, Selmer made just short of 1,000 guitars.

Mario Maccaferri was a talented guitarist and instrument designer, best known today for his Selmer-made guitars that were used so spectacularly by Django Reinhardt. Maccaferri was born in Italy in 1900. At the age of 11 he was apprenticed to instrument maker Luigi Mozzani, staying for 13 years. He began classical guitar studies at the prestigious Conservatory in Siena in 1916, receiving his diploma three years later. His career as a classical concert guitarist at first overshadowed his instrument making, but moving to London in 1929 he began teaching, and built himself an experimental guitar.

Maccaferri showed his homemade instrument to Selmer in London, which had been started in 1929 by saxophone player Ben Davis as a branch of the French Henri Selmer company. They liked Maccaferri's design, and set him up in the Selmer

factory near Paris to manufacture guitars, starting in 1932. The Selmer Maccaferri guitars were of unorthodox design, with a novel "flat" cutaway, enclosed tuners, and the option of an extra soundbox built inside the body, designed to increase sound projection through the guitar's distinctive "D" shape soundhole. Because of doubts over its effectiveness, the optional soundbox would later be dropped altogether.

A dispute led to Maccaferri's departure from Selmer in 1933, but the French company continued to manufacture Maccaferri-type guitars for another 19 years, switching to a 14th-fret neck joint in 1934, at which time the soundbox option was dropped and the soundhole shape was adapted to a smaller oval. After a swimming accident that halted his concert career, Maccaferri turned to manufacturing reeds for

◄ MACCAFERRI SHOWTIME

PRODUCED: *c1959-1969*

THIS EXAMPLE: *c1962*

BODY: *13" wide, 3⅛" deep*

Maccaferri produced quite a number of plastic guitar models during the 1950s and 1960s, although none was especially successful.

► MACCAFERRI ISLANDER 164A

PRODUCED: *c1954-1965*

THIS EXAMPLE: *c1959*

BODY: *12¾" wide, 3⅝" deep*

The Islander flat-top, like the G-40 shown far left, had a tailpiece that recalled Maccaferri's Selmer guitars. The Islander shown had an "ivory" body and "ebony" fingerboard.

◄ MACCAFERRI NEW ROMANCER

PRODUCED: *c1957-1965*

THIS EXAMPLE: *c1960*

BODY: *12⅜" wide, 3¼" deep*

The most decorated of Maccaferri's plastic guitars, the Romancer was splattered with scenes of groovy guys and gals just itching to make music with their brand new plastic axes. The Romancer, claimed a Maccaferri ad of the time, was "very easy to play, and luxuriously finished – the ideal guitar for any type of music, from classical to popular, folksong, calypso, rock'n'roll, etc."

wind instruments, and emigrated to the United States in 1939 to continue this business. By 1940 he was making plastic reeds, and plastic instruments followed, with enormously successful plastic ukuleles from 1949 – nine million were sold over 20 years – and guitars in 1953. The plastic guitars were surprisingly good, but sold in nothing like the quantities of the ukuleles. Production trickled on until the end of the 1960s, and Mario Maccaferri died in 1993, at the age of 92. Michael Wright wrote in *Vintage Guitar*: "Mario Maccaferri contributed mightily to the guitar cause over the course of the 20th century, as a trailblazing classical guitarist, award-winning luthier, plastics innovator, and father of the plastic guitar."

Good instruments, low prices and stylish ads were not enough to make Maccaferri plastic guitars a success.

▼ **GRETSCH WHITE PENGUIN**

PRODUCED: *1956–c1961*

THIS EXAMPLE: *c1956; serial 20573*

BODY: *13½" wide, 2" deep*

Unveiled at a trade show in 1956 and then made in very small numbers, the White Penguin *is a rare creature indeed. The original owner paid about $450 for this one, fooled around with it for a few months, and then put it under the bed. Forty years later when he took it out it had appreciated to $60,000! Many collectors covet a* Penguin *for its mystique, its rarity, and its unique aura.*

1956

GRETSCH RELEASES THE WHITE PENGUIN

In the wake of the luxurious White Falcon model, Gretsch makes a very small number of a semi-solid companion guitar, the White Penguin.

After the war, Gretsch moved from being a jobber (or distributor) and manufacturer of musical instruments primarily for other companies to an emphasis on the Gretsch brand. So it was that in the late 1940s the company introduced Gretsch drums, and by 1950 had established new Gretsch acoustic and electric guitars. Jimmie Webster, a talented musician and piano tuner, was hired by Gretsch to promote and manage the new guitar lines.

Over the following years Webster became Gretsch's main guitar ideas man, devising all manner of guitar models such as the White Falcon and add-on gadgets like the Space

Control bridge and stereo circuitry, as well as encouraging the spread of colored finishes from drum shells to guitar bodies. Webster also traveled far and wide to promote Gretsch guitars in "Guitarama" shows, as well as demonstrating to guitar-hungry audiences his

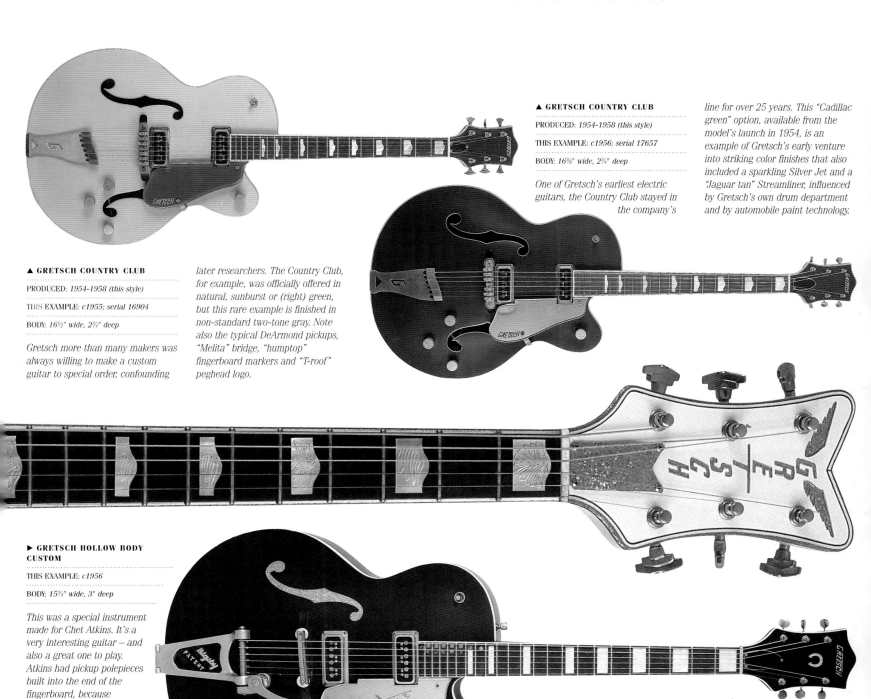

▲ **GRETSCH COUNTRY CLUB**

PRODUCED: *1954-1958 (this style)*

THIS EXAMPLE: *c1956; serial 17657*

BODY: *16⅜" wide, 2¾" deep*

One of Gretsch's earliest electric guitars, the Country Club stayed in the company's line for over 25 years. This "Cadillac green" option, available from the model's launch in 1954, is an example of Gretsch's early venture into striking color finishes that also included a sparkling Silver Jet and a "Jaguar tan" Streamliner, influenced by Gretsch's own drum department and by automobile paint technology.

▲ **GRETSCH COUNTRY CLUB**

PRODUCED: *1954-1958 (this style)*

THIS EXAMPLE: *c1955; serial 16904*

BODY: *16½" wide, 2¾" deep*

Gretsch more than many makers was always willing to make a custom guitar to special order, confounding later researchers. The Country Club, for example, was officially offered in natural, sunburst or (right) green, but this rare example is finished in non-standard two-tone gray. Note also the typical DeArmond pickups, "Melita" bridge, "humptop" fingerboard markers and "T-roof" peghead logo.

▶ **GRETSCH HOLLOW BODY CUSTOM**

THIS EXAMPLE: *c1956*

BODY: *15¾" wide, 3" deep*

This was a special instrument made for Chet Atkins. It's a very interesting guitar – and also a great one to play. Atkins had pickup polepieces built into the end of the fingerboard, because he wanted to run them through a separate octave multiplier to create low, soft bass tones. Also worth noting is the dark color, which is unique to this model, as are the sparkle-finish f-hole infills.

▲ **GRETSCH WHITE FALCON STEREO**

PRODUCED: *1958-1959 (this style)*

THIS EXAMPLE: *c1958; serial 26334*

BODY: *13¼" wide, 2" deep*

Witness the class and elegance of the classic Falcon. This is another example of a non-standard Gretsch: the control layout is of the 1958-59 stereo version, but pickup placement is like a mono Falcon of the period.

unusual "Touch System" of playing, a sort of early tapping style. Webster is summed up by the authors of *The Gretsch Book* like this: "He was a great find for Gretsch: a musician, an inventor and a salesman all wrapped up in one likable, outgoing personality. He probably did more than anyone else to spread the word about Gretsch guitars, and became a traveling ambassador for Gretsch, for electric guitars, and for guitar playing in general."

One of the most important connections that Webster made for Gretsch was to introduce guitar star Chet Atkins to the company in the early 1950s. Gretsch benefited enormously, not just from a line of fine Chet Atkins models, but from the endorsement of one of the best known and most respected players of the day. It was also no hardship when Beatle George Harrison adopted a Gretsch Chet Atkins Country Gentleman for many of the group's most visible live shows in the 1960s. Webster's most famous design for Gretsch was the gleaming White Falcon, as well as its rare, shortlived "solidbody" companion, the White Penguin.

The Falcon was a spectacular object, apparently made at first to dazzle visitors to a trade show but soon in demand as a production item. "An instrument for the artist-player whose caliber justifies and demands the utmost in striking beauty, luxurious styling and peak tonal performance and who is willing to pay the price," said Gretsch's publicity of its $600 masterpiece. Soon afterwards came a semi-solidbody version, the rare, highly collectible White Penguin.

1957

KAY CREATES THE NEW BARNEY KESSEL MODEL

In an image-enhancing deal, the usually budget conscious Kay company launches a line of three upscale guitars endorsed by the leading jazz guitarist of the day, Barney Kessel, best known for his stylish "Poll Winners" recordings. While Kessel apparently does not feel the need actually to go so far as to use the guitars on stage or in the studio, these striking, well made instruments do Kay's reputation no harm at all.

▼ KAY BARNEY KESSEL PRO

PRODUCED: *1957-1960*

THIS EXAMPLE: *c1958*

BODY: *13" wide, 2⅞" deep*

Kay made three shortlived Barney Kessel models during the 1950s: the

Jazz Special, which at $400 was Kay's most expensive guitar at the time; the $300 Artist (see above); and the $200 Pro, seen here. The Pro was of semi-solid construction with a maple top, as opposed to the hollow-body Artist and Jazz Special which each had a spruce top.

Kay had its origins in 1890 in a company called Groehsl, which by 1921 had become known as Stromberg-Voisinet (and was unrelated to Boston archtop maker Stromberg). By the mid 1920s the main influence in the company was its treasurer, Henry Kay Kuhrmeyer, whose middle name would later gain significance. Kuhrmeyer expanded Stromberg-Voisinet greatly during the late 1920s, taking on contract work for Montgomery Ward and Regal among others.

The Kay Kraft line of higher grade instruments was introduced in March 1931, and by the end of that year the name of the company was changed from Stromberg-Voisinet to Kay Musical Instruments, based on Walnut Street in Chicago. Kuhrmeyer eventually sold Kay in 1955 to a group of investors including Sidney Katz, who had been a manager at

▼ **KAY BARNEY KESSEL ARTIST**

PRODUCED: *1957-1960*

THIS EXAMPLE: *c1958*

BODY: *16" wide, 3½" deep*

In an effort to reverse its downscale image, Kay announced "with deep pride" in 1957: "Kay and the nation's number one jazz guitarist

Barney Kessel, winner of the Down Beat, Metronome and Playboy polls, have together developed a professional guitar which will establish new standards in quality of sound, workmanship and design." The overall effect is fun, especially the injection-molded plastic "Kelvinator" peghead that looks like that company's refrigerator logo.

▲ **KAY JAZZ II K776**

PRODUCED: *1961-1965*

THIS EXAMPLE: *c1962*

BODY: *15" wide, 1⅞" deep*

Retaining the Kay Kessel models' wonderful peghead (although this type with black facing is known as the "semi-Kelvinator") and the company's distinctive "bat wing" pickguard, the Jazz II was a stylish take on the currently hip double-cutaway thinline body design. A similar guitar to the example shown was used at least once during 1963 by a young Eric Clapton in one of his earliest groups, The Roosters.

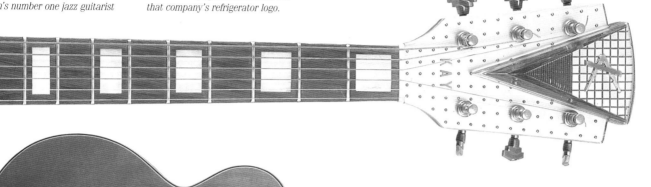

▲ **OLD KRAFTSMAN "CROWN"**

PRODUCED: *c1940-1942*

THIS EXAMPLE: *c1941*

BODY: *15½" wide, 4" deep*

Kay made this guitar for Spiegel, a large Chicago mail-order house that used the Old Kraftsman brand for its merchandise. Over the years Kay, along with manufacturers such as

Danelectro and Harmony, would produce many such "catalog" guitars, including instruments for Montgomery Ward (Airline) and Sears (Silvertone). This was probably the top of Spiegel's Old Kraftsman line in the early 1940s, with fancy fingerboard inlays, attractive back decal (left) and "crown" soundhole. (The tailpiece of this example is not original.)

▶ **KAY K40**

PRODUCED: *c1941-1942*

THIS EXAMPLE: *c1941*

BODY: *17" wide, 3½" deep*

A fine example of Kay's better early work, this K40 model has an unusual "two tone" fingerboard, with a contrasting wooden inlay running its full length. The model did not survive the war, although the similar K42 appeared in the late 1940s but without the eccentric fingerboard.

▲ **KAY UP-BEAT K8995J**

PRODUCED: *c1960-1961 (this style)*

THIS EXAMPLE: *c1960*

BODY: *17" wide, 2⅝" deep*

Issued with one or two pickups in 1958, the Upbeat line gained this three-pickup model in 1960 when it appeared in Kay's catalog at $225.

the other big Chicago guitar company of the time, Harmony. Katz became president of Kay, and gradually turned the company into another Harmony, primarily making less expensive student instruments of average quality, although as we see on these pages there were notable exceptions.

As usual, Kay made its own lines but also continued to supply a great number of instruments to other companies, especially the mail-order outfits such as Sears. "Badge-engineered" versions of Kay models would be sold by Sears,

for example the Kay Thin Twin electric which was offered by Sears under its in-house Silvertone brand. By 1960 Kay had become one of the largest guitar producers in America.

Guitar historian Mike Newton: "Katz built a huge new factory in the Chicago suburb of Elk Grove Village in 1963, just in time to get walloped by the first wave of Japanese import guitars. So Kay, heavily in debt over the new factory, was sold in 1965 to Seeburg, the Chicago juke box manufacturer. During 1967, Seeburg sold Kay to Valco (see p.106). The slump in guitar sales of the late 1960s hit Kay hard, and creditors closed down the factory in 1968, an action that effectively destroyed both Kay and Valco." The Kay brandname was subsequently sold, and was revived on a line of imported guitars, which is where it still resides today.

1957

GIBSON ACQUIRES THE EPIPHONE COMPANY

Gibson buys Epiphone for its double-bass business, but soon realizes that the company's guitars are much more important, and launches a revitalized line in 1958.

▲ **EPIPHONE ZEPHYR EMPEROR REGENT**

PRODUCED: *1950-1958*

THIS EXAMPLE: *1953; serial 67926*

BODY: *18½" wide, 3½" deep*

Before being acquired by Gibson in 1957, Epiphone had four years

earlier moved from its old New York base to Philadelphia. The luxuriously named Zephyr Emperor Regent was the flagship electric model of the time, complete with three pickups and Epiphone's six-button "color tone" system (see inset close-up) that gives a variety of pickup combinations. This Zephyr has pickups made by the Rowe DeArmond company, rather than Epiphone's own "New York" pickups, presumably one of the cost-cutting victims of the operation's move to Philadelphia during 1953.

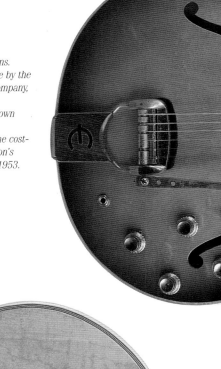

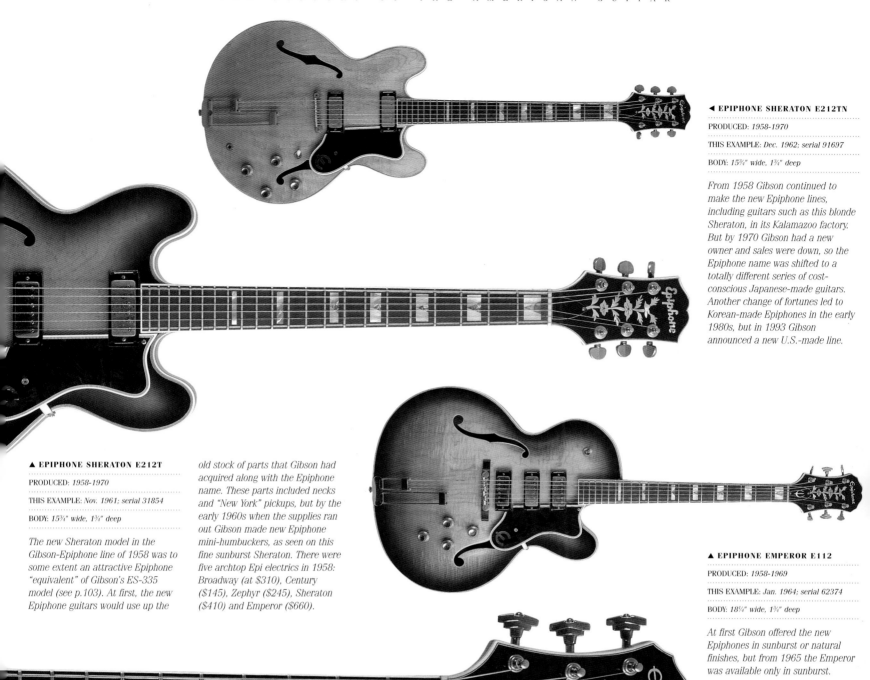

◄ **EPIPHONE SHERATON E212TN**

PRODUCED: *1958-1970*

THIS EXAMPLE: *Dec. 1962; serial 91697*

BODY: *15¾" wide, 1¾" deep*

From 1958 Gibson continued to make the new Epiphone lines, including guitars such as this blonde Sheraton, in its Kalamazoo factory. But by 1970 Gibson had a new owner and sales were down, so the Epiphone name was shifted to a totally different series of cost-conscious Japanese-made guitars. Another change of fortunes led to Korean-made Epiphones in the early 1980s, but in 1993 Gibson announced a new U.S.-made line.

▲ **EPIPHONE SHERATON E212T**

PRODUCED: *1958-1970*

THIS EXAMPLE: *Nov. 1961; serial 31854*

BODY: *15¾" wide, 1¾" deep*

The new Sheraton model in the Gibson-Epiphone line of 1958 was to some extent an attractive Epiphone "equivalent" of Gibson's ES-335 model (see p.103). At first, the new Epiphone guitars would use up the

old stock of parts that Gibson had acquired along with the Epiphone name. These parts included necks and "New York" pickups, but by the early 1960s when the supplies ran out Gibson made new Epiphone mini-humbuckers, as seen on this fine sunburst Sheraton. There were five archtop Epi electrics in 1958: Broadway (at $310), Century ($145), Zephyr ($245), Sheraton ($410) and Emperor ($660).

▲ **EPIPHONE EMPEROR E112**

PRODUCED: *1958-1969*

THIS EXAMPLE: *Jan. 1964; serial 62374*

BODY: *18¼" wide, 1¾" deep*

At first Gibson offered the new Epiphones in sunburst or natural finishes, but from 1965 the Emperor was available only in sunburst.

▲ **EPIPHONE EMPEROR E112TN**

PRODUCED: *1958-1969*

THIS EXAMPLE: *1963; serial 62350*

BODY: *18⅛" wide, 1¾" deep*

While the name certainly dated back to Epiphone's New York days – an Emperor archtop acoustic had first been offered by the company in the mid 1930s – Gibson's new electric version had a thinline body, which was certainly unlike anything that the tradition-based Epiphone had produced. Gibson also disposed of the electric Emperor's distinctive six-button pickup control panel, replacing it with conventional "two and two" volume and tone knobs.

The Epiphone company had experienced a number of complicated business maneuvers around 1950, and some control had been passed to Continental, the distribution division of C. G. Conn of Elkhart, Indiana, in 1948. Continental moved Epiphone production from New York to Philadelphia in 1953 after failing to resolve union dissent at the old plant.

A good deal of the Epiphone workforce did not make the move, and instead many of them were happily taken on by the new Guild company that had been started in New York in 1952 by Alfred Dronge and George Mann. A number of the early Guild models bear unmistakable marks of Epiphone-style craftsmanship, including the very distinctive "V-block" pearl fingerboard markers. Epiphone struggled on without many of the workers who had made the company's great archtops of

earlier years, while members of the founding Stathopoulo family were in disarray – Epi had died in 1943, and Frixo sold out to Orphie Stathopoulo in 1948.

Epiphone looked close to imploding on itself by the mid 1950s, and in 1957 Gibson agreed to buy the faltering operation. According to Gibson's president at the time, Ted McCarty, Gibson thought that for the $20,000 asking price they were buying Epiphone's double-bass business, but it got a small stock of Epiphone guitar parts as well.

McCarty decided that, in addition to the basses he'd been so keen to acquire in the first place, Gibson would also produce a new line of Epiphone guitars so that the oversubscribed demand for Gibson dealerships could be satisfied with a fresh new alternative.

1957

D'ANGELICO DESIGNS AND BUILDS THE "TEARDROP"

After a local nightclub guitarist asks John D'Angelico to make him an instrument that audiences will remember, the great guitar maker comes up with one of the most outlandish and spectacular guitar designs ever, the unique D'Angelico Teardrop. This remarkable example of the luthier's art becomes one of the most valuable and desirable musical instruments in the world.

These unique photographs (left) were taken in the D'Angelico workshop in 1957 as the Teardrop was built, and marked a notable event: it was the only guitar that D'Angelico ever made where he deviated from his standard guitar shape, and was by far the fanciest guitar he ever built. Peter Girardi is the man pictured in the dark jacket, while John D'Angelico is the balding gent with the charming striped underwear.

▶ D'AQUISTO SOLO "TEARDROP"

THIS EXAMPLE: *Aug. 1993; serial 1246*

BODY: *17½" wide, 3⅛" deep*

Jimmy D'Aquisto worked with John D'Angelico when the original Teardrop was made back in the late 1950s, and in fact it was D'Aquisto who first alerted guitar-collector Scott Chinery to the fact that the D'Angelico Teardrop existed. Chinery started to get to know D'Aquisto in the early 1990s, and in 1993 he suggested that D'Aquisto might like to build a new Teardrop, but in terms of and based on D'Aquisto's own design ideas. That was the genesis of the D'Aquisto guitar that you see here (plus the original "form," inset). The Teardrop that D'Aquisto made for Chinery used a different approach than the original: this guitar has a much more refined, open, harp-like sound, more or less the antithesis of the D'Angelico approach. Chinery's view was that the D'Angelico Teardrop isn't "better" than the D'Aquisto: it was more the case that each guitar represented a pinnacle in the career of its individual creator and stands on its own merits.

John D'Angelico ran his workshop on Kenmare Street, New York, where he had been making and repairing guitars and mandolins since the early 1930s. Soon D'Angelico had begun to make his own mark and started refining his instruments, and jazz players in particular were drawn to D'Angelico's big, powerful guitars and their distinctive sound and presence.

Even though D'Angelico had by 1936 started to define his two most famous models, the New Yorker and the Excel, features and appointments were never too precise, and D'Angelico would adapt and modify the instruments, within certain guidelines, but pretty much as he or his customer chose. Operating effectively as a custom shop, where instruments were made to each individual order rather than on a strictly defined model basis, D'Angelico's business inevitably veered from the mainstream instruments that helped him to make his living as a respected guitar maker. So if one of his customers wanted some particular repair work done, then of course D'Angelico would oblige. And if a player wanted a D'Angelico neck put onto an existing body from another guitar maker, then that too would be viewed philosophically as a way of bringing in extra dollars to the Kenmare Street workshop.

But one day in 1957 D'Angelico received the strangest request ever for a custom guitar. Into the shop walked one Peter Girardi, a local player who worked as a musical entertainer in various nightclubs in the neighborhood. He wanted a guitar that customers would remember, he told

▼ FENDER JAZZMASTER

PRODUCED: 1958-1980, 1986-current

THIS EXAMPLE: 1960; serial 61971

BODY: 13¾" wide, 1" deep

A switch above the Jazzmaster's fingerboard selected between a rhythm circuit, which could be set with the two roller controls nearby, and a lead circuit, controlled by the two conventional knobs. There was also a standard pickup selector. Fiesta Red, seen here and one of Fender's first custom colors, was originally made by Du Pont for the 1956 Ford Thunderbird. Fender employee George Fullerton says that a year or two later he had a Fiesta Red sample made up at a paint store near the Fender factory and applied it to a Jazzmaster prototype – apparently the first Fender finished in the color. Other examples of Fender's custom colors are shown on the collection of Jazzmasters pictured on the right-hand page.

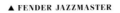

▲ FENDER JAZZMASTER

PRODUCED: 1958-1980, 1986-current

THIS EXAMPLE: 1962; serial 89171

BODY: 13¾" wide, 1" deep

Here's a classic example of how Fender's "clear" lacquer applied over the color coat can yellow with age and distort the look of the original color. This Jazzmaster probably started life with a Blue Ice Metallic custom color. However, more than 30 years of an unavoidable "yellowing" of its outer skin has transformed this instrument's finish into what is nevertheless a very attractive green color.

▲ FENDER JAZZMASTER

PRODUCED: 1958-1980, 1986-current

THIS EXAMPLE: 1966; serial 178685

BODY: 13¾" wide, 1" deep

The paints used by Fender for their custom-color instruments originated in automobile manufacturing. For example, Fender called the copper-like shade seen on this particualr Jazzmaster "Shoreline Gold", copying the name that Pontiac had employed for a car during the late 1950s. The same color was also known as "Golden Mist", by Oldsmobile, and "Pearl Fawn" when used by Buick.

Gretsch had first hit on the idea of using paints made by Du Pont, the biggest supplier of paint to the auto companies, and Fender followed in the later 1950s.

Fender had sold the occasional guitar finished in a non-standard solid color from about 1954, but two years later offered official "player's choice" colors on its pricelist (for a five per cent surcharge). In 1957 Fender came up with the name "custom colors," a term that has stuck ever since, and even issued color charts in the early 1960s. Fender used a variety of Du Pont lacquers – some from the company's Duco nitro-cellulose lines, such as Dakota Red, others from the Lucite acrylics, like Burgundy Mist Metallic. Over the color, a final nitro-cellulose-based clear lacquer was usually added.

Original custom-color Fenders are now very collectible, but excellent "refinishes" abound, while identifying specific colors can be tricky. The "clear" lacquer can yellow with age, which for example might turn an original blue into more of a green. With the reds the problem is fading, due to a reaction to sunlight. This has led some collectors to invent bogus names that never existed as official Fender colors, such as "salmon pink" or "coral pink" to describe a faded guitar that started as a vibrant Fiesta Red. As experienced custom-color researcher Clay Harrell reflects: "Few things in the vintage guitar market are so confusing as Fender custom color guitars."

1958

FENDER LAUNCHES ITS NEW JAZZMASTER MODEL

In a bid to widen the appeal of solidbody electric guitars amid the more refined air of the jazz guitarist, Fender issues a new deluxe instrument, the Jazzmaster. At the same time, the company is expanding the scope and availability of an official line of vibrant "custom colors" on many of its guitars, including the Jazzmaster.

▼ FENDER JAZZMASTER

PRODUCED: *1958-1980, 1986-current*

THIS EXAMPLE: *1958; serial 026525*

BODY: *13¾" wide, 1" deep*

This is one of several prototypes for the Jazzmaster. It has some features that did not make the production examples, such as the blackcove_ pickups, black pickguard, a_d bl_ vibrato plate, and it has a Stratocaster neck. This is d_ted _ 1958, implying that this ma_ hav_ been one of the samples ta_en t_ publicize the new model at _at year's trade show. (The Fen_er d_ on the peghead was added l_ter._

The new Fender Jazzmaster took over from the Stratocaster as the California company's top-of-the-line solidbody electric model when it was introduced during 1958, four years after the Strat had appeared. At $329.50 on the July 1958 pricelist, the Jazzmaster was definitely an upscale guitar, pitched at $55 more than a vibrato-equipped Strat, although it was a little cheaper than Gibson's most expensive solidbody of the time, the Les Paul Custom, which listed at $375.

Fender's intention, evident from the model name, was for the new Jazzmaster to attract jazz players, but in fact there was little about the Fender guitar to entice conservative jazz guitarists away from the refined tones of their hollow-body Gibsons. The Jazzmaster had an odd "lock-off" facility on its new-design vibrato, as well as big, wide pickups that seemed

to invite hum and noise, and relatively complex electrics – independent circuits were offered so that the player coul_ up a lead sound and a rhythm sound and then switch betw_ them. All this did little to enthuse any kind of player, let a_ jazzmen. In the 1960s, Bob Bogle of instrumental pop b_ The Ventures would help improve the Jazzmaster's image_ would later new-wavers like Elvis Costello, Robert Smit_ The Cure and Tom Verlaine of Television.

It was also around the time of the Jazzmast_ introduction in 1958 that Fender's "custom colors" bega_ move into the spotlight. The automobile business ha_ profound effect on U.S. guitar design in the 1950s, not lea_ legitimizing the art of industrial form, but also in enhan_ an already stylish object with a rich and vivid paint fi_

backshot (above) demonstrates
mor clearly the flowing,
nt bdy curves of D'Angelico's
off Tardrop guitar design.

▼ **D'ANGELICO NEW YORKER
CUTAWAY SPECIAL –
"THE TEARDROP"**

THIS EXAMPLE: *Jun. 1957: serial 2032*

BODY: *17½" wide, 3¼" deep*

*Even before anyone had even seen
this instrument, collectors knew that
it existed: it was one of those
enigmatic "out there somewhere"
guitars. When it surfaced, everyone
interested in vintage guitars felt a
buzz of excitement. Inside the*

*guitar on the back are a number of
interesting inscriptions. The main
one reads: "Specially designed and
made for Mr. Peter Girardi" and it's
then signed by John D'Angelico and
dated June 18th 1957. It has two
serial numbers: D'Angelico's
sequential #2032, as well as a
special #1 stamped separately. Peter
Girardi was a nightclub performer
who wanted something his audiences
would always remember. He certainly
got it! But little did he know that the
design would also have a sonic*

*importance: it really does open up
the sound, and it's one of the most
powerful archtop guitars you're likely
to hear. When Scott Chinery bought
the Teardrop for $150,000 it was the
highest price ever paid for a "non-
celebrity" guitar. Quite what the
guitar's value is today is open to
speculation. But what remains
certain is that the D'Angelico
Teardrop is among the best known
and most prestigious vintage guitars,
and it will surely always be revered
by makers, players, and collectors.*

*Also shown here (below) is a back
shot of the D'Aquisto Teardrop that
demonstrates the maker's expertise
in selecting first-grade timbers for
his guitars. In this case, it seems
that D'Aquisto excelled even his own
especially high standards.*

D'Angelico: something that would make Girardi stick in the
audience's minds and, hopefully, keep them coming back so
that his employers would continue to book him.

D'Angelico worked hard to come up with a design that
would fit Girardi's request. Eventually, he devised a New
Yorker-type guitar, but with an extra projection from the lower
half of the body to create what he called a "can opener" shape,
pushing the body out to a pointed tip on the lower bout.

One can almost hear D'Angelico saying, "Well, Peter,
they sure will remember *this* guitar!" Years later, the
guitar would turn up and be purchased by Scott
Chinery, who in 1993 had D'Angelico's protégé Jimmy
D'Aquisto build a modern reinterpretation of the unique guitar
that has come to be known as the D'Angelico Teardrop.

▲ JAZZMASTER Olympic White

THIS EXAMPLE: 1962; serial 78707

▲ JAZZMASTER non-standard blue sparkle

THIS EXAMPLE: 1961; serial 67236

▲ JAZZMASTER Sonic Blue

THIS EXAMPLE: 1962; serial 85699

▲ JAZZMASTER Foam Green

THIS EXAMPLE: 1963; serial L19800

▲ JAZZMASTER Sunburst

THIS EXAMPLE: 1960; serial 62217

▲ JAZZMASTER Blonde

THIS EXAMPLE: 1959; serial 32203

▲ JAZZMASTER Candy Apple Red

THIS EXAMPLE: 1962; serial 80110

▲ JAZZMASTER Sherwood Green Metallic

THIS EXAMPLE: 1966; serial 130445

▲ JAZZMASTER Blonde (gold hardware)

THIS EXAMPLE: 1961; serial 59550

▲ JAZZMASTER Lake Placid Blue Metallic

THIS EXAMPLE: 1963; serial L22178

▲ JAZZMASTER Black

THIS EXAMPLE: 1960; serial 52521

▲ JAZZMASTER Sunburst (anodized 'guard)

THIS EXAMPLE: 1959; serial 38155

▲ JAZZMASTER Burgundy Mist Metallic

THIS EXAMPLE: 1961; serial 72863

▲ JAZZMASTER Dakota Red

THIS EXAMPLE: 1961; serial 67474

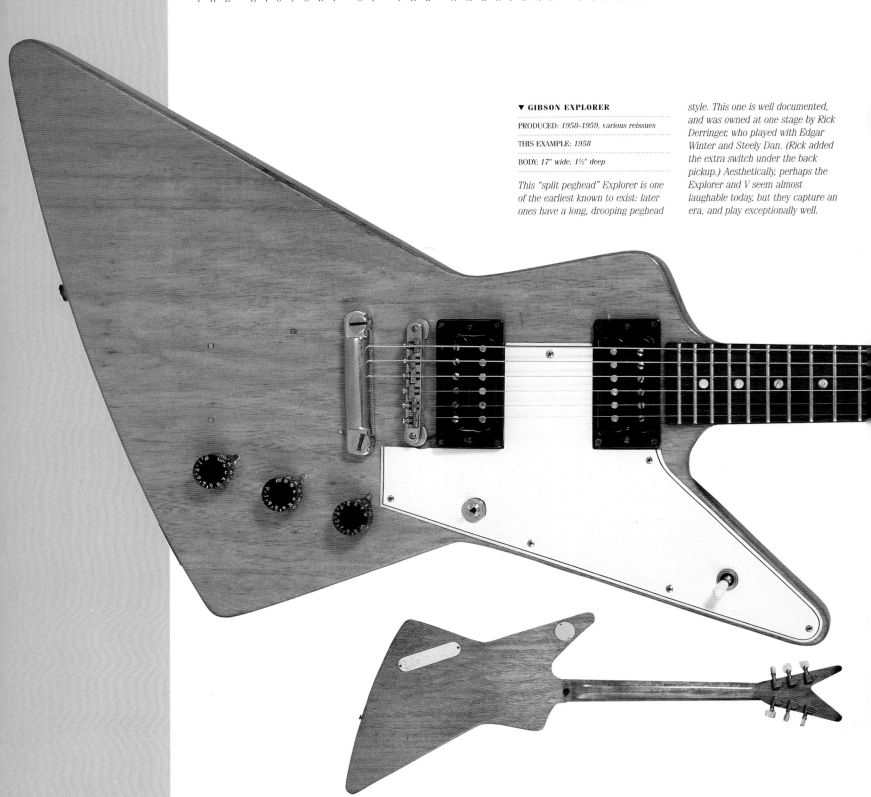

▼ **GIBSON EXPLORER**

PRODUCED: *1958-1959, various reissues*

THIS EXAMPLE: *1958*

BODY: *17" wide, 1½" deep*

This "split peghead" Explorer is one of the earliest known to exist: later ones have a long, drooping peghead style. This one is well documented, and was owned at one stage by Rick Derringer, who played with Edgar Winter and Steely Dan. (Rick added the extra switch under the back pickup.) Aesthetically, perhaps the Explorer and V seem almost laughable today, but they capture an era, and play exceptionally well.

1958

GIBSON ADDS EXPLORER, FLYING V AND ES-335

In a classic year of innovation and experiment, Gibson unleashes a sublime semi-solid model and a wild pair of angular "Modernistic" instruments.

Gibson introduced two new lines during 1958, one of which was of clear importance right from the start, while the other failed at the time and only later grew in significance.

The Gibson "Modernistic" guitars were first seen in public during 1958. Fender's more flamboyant designs such as the Stratocaster and the new-in-1958 Jazzmaster had been leaving Gibson's rather staid solidbody models behind in the midst of the rise of rock'n'roll, when guitar makers became increasingly aware, in addition to the usual considerations of quality and playability, of the value of visual appeal.

So the designers at Gibson temporarily set aside their customary preoccupation with curvaceously elegant forms, and came up with the boldly adventurous Flying V and Explorer, a pair of stark, linear creations. "An asset to the combo musician with a flair for showmanship," insisted Gibson, urging: "Dealers, try one of these 'new look' instruments – either is a sure-fire hit with guitarists of today!" But customers ignored the designs as too futuristic and un-Gibson, and the small numbers produced would turn the Modernistics into future collectibles of the rarest kind.

A much more successful Gibson innovation of 1958 was the evidently inventive company's new ES-335 guitar, a development of its thin-body "thinline" design that had begun with models such as the Byrdland and the ES-350T in 1955. With the 335, however, the company deployed a radical double-cutaway style, as well as a novel solid block within the otherwise hollow body to create a new "semi-solid" structure. Gibson's idea was effectively to combine a hollow-body guitar

▲ GIBSON FLYING V

PRODUCED: *1958-1959, various reissues*

THIS EXAMPLE: *1959; serial 9 0932*

BODY: *16¾" wide, 1⅜" deep*

Imagine what players must have thought of these when they came out! Actually, nobody liked Gibson's radical new "Modernistic" style back then. Only 98 Flying Vs were officially shipped by Gibson in the 1950s, and despite a less than clear factory record it is thought that no more than 22 Explorers left the factory at the same time. So these are now super-rare collectible guitars and some of the highest value instruments on the market.

▼ GIBSON ES-335TN

PRODUCED: *1958-1982*

THIS EXAMPLE: *Nov. 1959; serial A31554*

BODY: *16" wide, 1¾" deep*

The classic 335 is this "dot neck" type, named for fingerboard dot-shape markers used until 1962 (when "blocks" were introduced). A shorter pickguard came in 1961; the stop-tailpiece was withdrawn in '64.

▲ GIBSON ES-335T

PRODUCED: *1958-1982*

THIS EXAMPLE: *May 1959; serial A30219*

BODY: *15¾" wide, 1¾" deep*

At first Gibson's ES-335 was offered in sunburst ($267.50) or natural finish ($282.50), with cherry red officially introduced during 1960. But some rare cherry 335s do occur

before that date, as demonstrated by this fine 1959 example. A good proportion of Gibson electrics of the period were fitted at the factory with Bigsby vibratos, and on 335-type guitars this meant that the holes already drilled for the normal tailpiece would be filled either with pearl dots (as this example) or with a black plate marked "Custom Made" (see the ES-345 on p.105).

▼ GIBSON L-5CT

PRODUCED: *1958-1961*

THIS EXAMPLE: *Dec. 1958; serial A28686*

BODY: *16¾" wide, 2¼" deep*

First made in March 1958 especially for comedian "Lonesome" George Gobel, this acoustic thinline was an unusual design combination.

with a solidbody, not only in terms of construction but also in sonic effect. A problem for hollow-body guitars was the screeching feedback that often occurred when the guitar was played at high volume. The 335's solid maple block inside the "wonder-thin" body tamed the feedback and combined pure solidbody sustain with the "woody" warmth of a hollow-body.

This quality would endear the 335 to a wide range of players, from bluesman B. B. King to jazz stylist Larry Carlton. André Duchossoir sums up the innovative 335 in *Gibson Electrics – The Classic Years*: "There were a number of firsts in the early days of the electric guitar, but in retrospect only a few of them can be considered as true milestones. The double-cutaway thinlines pioneered by Gibson in 1958 genuinely rank amongst the greatest original designs."

◀ GIBSON ES-355TDSV

PRODUCED: *1959-1982*

THIS EXAMPLE: *Oct. 1960; serial A34868*

BODY: *16" wide, 1⅝" deep*

The ES-355, introduced in 1959, had the same double-cutaway, semi-solid body design of the previous year's innovative 335, but was an upscale version with better appointments and the option of stereo and Varitone circuits.

1959

GIBSON MAKES ITS FIRST STEREO GUITAR, THE ES-345

Taking careful note of the current proliferation of stereo recordings and electronic gadgetry, Gibson's electronics department goes into overdrive.

The possibility of a "stereo" guitar had originally been investigated by Jimmie Webster at Gretsch, who filed a patent for a stereo pickup system in 1956, leading to the company's as ever wonderfully titled Project-O-Sonic guitars of 1958 (for a White Falcon example, see p.90). Gibson's first take on the stereo idea, the ES-345, appeared in the following year.

"Stereophonic" and its more common diminutive, "stereo," had become buzzwords in the late 1950s, as first stereo pre-recorded tapes and then stereo records hit the market. Gretsch's pioneering system had worked by splitting each pickup on a two-pickup guitar effectively into two, so that one pickup feeds the output from the lower three strings to one amplifier, while the other pickup sends the higher three strings out to another amp. Gibson adopted a rather more straightforward system which debuted in 1959, at first on the new ES-345 and then the ES-355. This two-pickup circuitry simply directed the output of each complete pickup to a separate amplifier. In contemporary advertising, Gibson assured the guitarist of the day that it would soon be customary to plug in to a pair of amps and produce "a symphony of warm, full stereophonic sound."

Another new Gibson feature in the search for fresh electric tonalities was offered on the 345 and some ES-355s: the Varitone control, a switch that selected one of six preset tone options. But the Varitone and stereo capabilities were never especially popular among guitarists, who often disconnected the Varitone and, despite the stereo option, simply played what was a very good guitar in conventional "mono" mode.

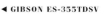

▼ GIBSON ES-355TDSV

PRODUCED: *1959-1982*

THIS EXAMPLE: *Oct. 1959; serial A31491*

BODY: *16" wide, 1¾" deep*

Nearly all 355s came in cherry red, such as the example shown at the

top of the opposite page. However, a small number were made in natural (see large guitar) or in cherry sunburst, like this rare example. Note that the person who custom-ordered it from Gibson in 1959 had his name, Steven O. Zollars, engraved onto the truss-rod cover.

◄ GIBSON ES-355TDSV

PRODUCED: *1959-1982*

THIS EXAMPLE: *1960; serial R2054*

BODY: *16" wide, 1⅝" deep*

This natural-finish 355 is the rarest guitar in an important group of Gibson 335-family instruments seen together on the pages of this book. To many players this design of Gibson electric is unique, offering a bluesy sound and feel that can be hard to duplicate on other instruments. This blonde-finish 355 is about as rare as it gets – it's generally thought that it may be one of only three in existence.

► GIBSON ES-335TDN SPECIAL

THIS EXAMPLE: *Oct. 1960; serial A34818*

BODY: *16" wide, 1¾" deep*

Another rare custom-ordered Gibson, this ES-335 has a fingerboard inlaid not with the dots one would expect on an example made between 1958 and 1962, but the "double parallelogram" markers usually associated with its stereo cousin, the ES-345 (see right).

▼ GIBSON ES-345TDSV

PRODUCED: *1959-1982*

THIS EXAMPLE: *Apr. 1963; serial 110878*

BODY: *16" wide, 1⅝" deep*

The ES-345 was Gibson's first stereo guitar. It had a circuit that, when connected to a suitable "Y"-cable, would split the pickups to two

individual amplifiers, creating a wide if not strictly stereo spread. It also had a Varitone six-way tone selector. By 1963, when this fine cherry example left the factory, the 335 family was priced as follows: the sunburst 335 was $300 ($315 in cherry); sunburst 345 was $395 ($410 cherry); and mono 355 was $595 ($645 with stereo and Varitone).

▼ NATIONAL NEWPORT 84

PRODUCED: *1963-1965*

THIS EXAMPLE: *1964; serial G22815*

BODY: *13¾" wide, 1½" deep*

In 1964 Valco had nine National "map shape" guitars on its pricelist, ranging from the wood-body Westwood 72 at $139.50 to the plastic-body Glenwood 99 at $450.

This plastic Newport 84, in "sea foam green," listed for $219.50. As well as its conventional magnetic pickup near the neck, the 84 like many of this series had an innovative "contact" pickup built into the bridge (note the connecting cable). The Newport models were fitted with National's own less-than-sturdy vibrato; the more expensive Glenwoods came with Bigsby units.

1962

VALCO INTRODUCES FIBERGLASS GUITARS

The renamed Valco company produces a striking line of molded fiberglass instruments, including the stylish National "map shape" models.

The National-Dobro company had, like most guitar makers, ceased operations during World War II, during which period National-Dobro was officially dissolved and the Valco Manufacturing Co. formed – merely a change of name, in effect. Business resumed after the war, and the products were still made in Chicago, bearing National, low-end Supro or one of the contract catalog-company brands such as Airline... but all now under the Valco banner. (For the National/Dobro story up to this point see National, p.39, and Dobro, p.42.) Valco was

▼ NATIONAL NEWPORT 82

PRODUCED: *1963-1965*

THIS EXAMPLE: *1964; serial G20912*

BODY: *13¾" wide, 1⅜" deep*

Valco's construction method for its fiberglass-reinforced plastic models of the 1950s is visible on this

"flame red" Newport example: the line of white vinyl binding around the body marks the point at which the two plastic molded halves were joined together. Collectors call the plastic Newports, Glenwoods and wooden Westwoods the "map shape" Nationals, because the body outline is supposed to resemble the shape of a map of the United States.

▲ SUPRO DUAL-TONE

PRODUCED: *1958-1960*

THIS EXAMPLE: *1958; serial X90937*

BODY: *13" wide, 1½" deep*

Valco's Supro brand was generally cheaper than National. Controls on this wood-body Dual-Tone include a volume and tone for each pickup.

► SUPRO BELMONT

PRODUCED: *1958-1960*

THIS EXAMPLE: *1960; serial T33040*

BODY: *12" wide, 1⅝" deep*

Here is Valco's earlier use of plastic: a conventional wooden body is "shrink-wrapped" in plastic, this one in a fetching red pearloid effect.

not the first brand to offer guitars built from synthetic materials: earlier innovations had, for example, included Rickenbacker's Bakelite models of the 1930s. But the brightly colored and unusually shaped fiberglass Valco-made guitars of the 1960s were without doubt among the most eye-catchingly different instruments of the era.

Valco was never short of impressive sounding names for its guitar innovations, and came up with "Res-O-Glas" and "Hollow-Glas" for the material used in its line of non-wood instruments. A more detailed description given at the time, "polyester resins with threads of pure glass," revealed the material as a fiberglass-reinforced plastic. Valco intended that this plastic material it had developed for its guitars would be

a more adaptable and workable medium than conventional wood, providing a longer lasting instrument. The company did continue to produce wooden-body models alongside the Res-O-Glas guitars, but the brave plastic experiment ended with Valco itself in the late 1960s. Valco bought the Kay guitar company in 1967, and when Kay went out of business during the following year, Valco went down with it.

But plastic would return to guitar making over the coming decades – for example with Ovation's round-backs, or modern carbon-fiber necks. Perhaps it will go further, too, as we concern ourselves about the ecological impact of depleting worldwide wood stocks. Some quality timbers are already scarce, and the search is on for "environmentally friendly" substitutes for nearly all the woods used in guitar making.

▲ NATIONAL VARSITY 66

PRODUCED: *1963-1965*

THIS EXAMPLE: *1964; serial G39844*

BODY: *13¼" wide, 1⅝" deep*

Although it's true to say that Supro was Valco's budget brand, some Nationals, like this $99.50 "jet black" plastic-body Varsity, did cross over into Supro territory. Usually, the brands can be simply identified by checking the shape of the peghead: National heads "point" to the right, Supros to the left.

◀ D'AQUISTO ELECTRIC

THIS EXAMPLE: c1965

BODY: 17" wide, 2¾" deep

It is said that this was the first guitar Jimmy D'Aquisto made on his own. Apparently it was on the table when his mentor, John D'Angelico, died. D'Aquisto eventually came back to the workshop and finished this instrument off, finally adding his own logo to the guitar's peghead.

1965

D'AQUISTO BEGINS MAKING GUITARS IN HIS OWN RIGHT

Following the death of John D'Angelico, with whom he had worked for 13 years, Jimmy D'Aquisto gradually starts to work on his own instruments. In time he introduces a series of new ideas, designs and styles that will eventually come to define the art of the modern archtop guitar.

After moving from the old D'Angelico workshop in Manhattan in the mid 1960s, Jimmy D'Aquisto (left) worked in a number of locations on Long Island, New York. At first he worked out of Huntington, then Farmingdale, and finally D'Aquisto settled his shop in Greenport, out at the eastern end of the island, around 1990. He is seen in these three photos (left) in his workshop during the mid-1980s, posing for the camera while apparently working on a body rim (far left), adjusting a neck (center) and proudly holding an instrument that is close to completion. As far as his working methods and materials were concerned, he once told Paul

Schmidt: "I'm not an expert on the detailed scientific structures of the wood – I never even consider that. Art is not confined to the rules. The people with the theories can rarely build anything. There are no definite rules to my method of creating an instrument. I build upon the ideas I learned in the beginning with John [D'Angelico] and, since his death, the discoveries I make with my own instruments." D'Aquisto continued: "I always tried to put all I believed into my work. It can only work if one strives to better oneself. I never tried to be better than John: he was D'Angelico trying to make a D'Angelico guitar; I am D'Aquisto and I'm making my guitar."

◄ D'AQUISTO NEW YORKER SPECIAL

PRODUCED: c1966-1995

THIS EXAMPLE: Mar. 1978; serial 1120

BODY: 17" wide, 3⅛" deep

D'Aquisto's New Yorker Special was his 17-inch archtop model. This example shows the changes he had made since its D'Angelico roots, including "S"-shape soundholes (since the late 1960s) and an ebony tailpiece (since the early 1970s).

▼ D'AQUISTO NEW YORKER OVAL HOLE

PRODUCED: c1972-1973

THIS EXAMPLE: Mar. 1973; serial 1068

BODY: 16¾" wide, 3⅛" deep

D'Aquisto explained his passion for oval soundholes by likening the effect to a squeezed garden hose; the sound, like the water in the hose, would come out more powerfully. Many people who met D'Aquisto discovered a remarkable man. Some describe an aura about him, and even those who didn't know him well felt they were in the presence of an extraordinary person. It's interesting that the innately talented D'Aquisto just happened to converge with the greatest guitar maker of the day. It seems now like a unique destiny.

▲ D'AQUISTO NEW YORKER CLASSIC

PRODUCED: 1985-1995

THIS EXAMPLE: Aug. 1986; serial 1191

BODY: 17" wide, 3" deep

In the late 1980s D'Aquisto developed the elegant Classic, with minimal binding and decoration, and largely wooden fittings. This one was originally owned by cult cartoonist and D'Aquisto fan Gary Larson. (Note that the date given for each D'Aquisto here is that written inside the guitar's back early in the production process; the guitar would be finished often months later.)

▶ D'AQUISTO NEW YORKER 7-STRING

PRODUCED: c1973-1984

THIS EXAMPLE: May 1975; serial 1093

BODY: 17" wide, 3" deep

D'Aquisto said once that he was unhappy making traditional guitars, though occasionally a player would order an unusual item such as this seven-string. D'Aquisto tried to break out for years, but he discovered that musicians are often conservative and surprisingly resistant to new ideas.

Jimmy D'Aquisto had first met the master instrument builder John D'Angelico while still in his teens, and would visit the Manhattan workshop after working during the day as a stockboy at a local department store. D'Aquisto's growing love for the guitar blossomed on those visits as he discovered the beautiful sounds that could come from an expertly crafted archtop instrument. Soon afterwards, D'Aquisto started working for D'Angelico, joining him and his assistant Vincent "Jimmy" DiSerio in Kenmare Street in 1951.

At first he would do odd jobs around the place, but D'Aquisto gradually began to learn about guitar making from D'Angelico and DiSerio. Around 1959 DiSerio left, and D'Aquisto became D'Angelico's assistant, taking on more of the general responsibility for the guitar building.

After a heart illness, D'Angelico died in 1964, and by the following year D'Aquisto was making guitars in his own right. At first these were D'Angelico-style instruments with "D'Aquisto" on the peghead, but gradually, and despite business difficulties following a hasty agreement D'Aquisto had made at the time, his own instruments began to appear.

D'Aquisto modified the D'Angelico style, steadily bringing more of his own ideas and designs into the archtop guitars he was building – first at the ex-D'Angelico workshop in Manhattan, then on Long Island, settling around 1990 in Greenport. Tragically, D'Aquisto, who suffered for years with epilepsy, died in 1995 at age 59 – ironically, the same early age at which his mentor, John D'Angelico, had died.

◀ **D'AQUISTO MANDOLIN**

THIS EXAMPLE: *Oct. 1972; serial 103*

BODY: *10⅜" wide, 1¾" deep*

It's interesting to follow the design of this instrument back to the Ciani mandolin (see p.55). At any rate, this is a rare instrument – D'Aquisto only ever made three mandolins.

D'Aquisto's best known guitars are the archtop instruments he made, and probably the most notable of all his guitars are the new, more adventurous designs he came up with during the last ten years of his life (see overleaf).

Perhaps less well known are D'Aquisto's flat-top guitars and his electric instruments, a selection of which is shown here. His flat-tops were mainly produced during the ten years or so from 1973. The story goes that the idea for a series of flat-tops developed soon after D'Aquisto had acquired some fine maple intended for use in the backs and sides of archtop instruments. But for technical reasons D'Aquisto decided that the new maple stock was actually more appropriate for flat-tops, and during the 1970s and into the 1980s he proceeded to make around 15 such guitars, with distinctive oval soundholes and, of course, the maple backs and sides. According to D'Aquisto's ledger, his flat-tops divide into three main models: the 15-inch non-cutaway Flat Top Special, the 15-inch cutaway Flat Top Small, and the 16-inch Delux. As usual these were just nominal guidelines, and D'Aquisto would customarily build to special order. One such notable commission came from singer-songwriter Janis Ian, who in 1981 ordered a flat-top from D'Aquisto, apparently intended to replace a stolen Martin D-18, although she ended up with a "typical" 16-inch flat-top with a special shorter body.

D'Aquisto's electric guitars at first had the contracted-out plywood bodies in the style of D'Angelico's electrics, but as time went on D'Aquisto got into a more individual style, as shown by the superb recent Centura Electric shown here.

▶ D'AQUISTO JAZZ MASTER

THIS EXAMPLE: *c1987*

BODY: *13¾" wide, 1¼" deep*

This "solidbody" electric actually has a solid central block in the body with hollow compartments either side. This design probably contributes to its beautifully warm sound.

▲ D'AQUISTO CENTURA ELECTRIC

PRODUCED: *c1991-1995*

THIS EXAMPLE: *Dec. 1991; serial 1001*

BODY: *13¾" wide, 25½" deep*

D'Aquisto's electrics are interesting, none more so than this recent Centura, the electric version of the "later"-style guitars. In some ways it's designed for jazz more than rock: there are hollowed pockets inside, so the guitar doesn't sustain like a Les Paul, for example. It seems D'Aquisto was searching for a new kind of electric guitar with this design.

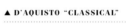

▲ D'AQUISTO "CLASSICAL"

THIS EXAMPLE: *Jan. 1982; serial 1*

BODY: *14¼" wide, 3⅞" deep*

D'Aquisto made very few classical nylon-string flat-tops, so this is a rare instrument. It's interesting that when D'Aquisto designed his later "futuristic" models (see overleaf), one of his major concerns was that they should be as versatile as possible, able to adapt to virtually any style the player intended. With this in mind he recommended that the steel-string archtops could also be set up to play with nylon strings, although few players have actually tried them that way. Perhaps one day it might seem perfectly natural to see a leading classical guitarist playing an archtop guitar?

▲ D'AQUISTO FLAT TOP DELUX

PRODUCED: *1976-1981*

THIS EXAMPLE: *Nov. 1977; serial 106*

BODY: *15¾" wide, 4⅜" deep*

Even when it came to flat-tops, which to all intents and purposes were something of a sideline to his main work building archtop guitars, D'Aquisto's flair for elegant design still shines through, as on this beautifully simple instrument. Customers talk of D'Aquisto's unmatched passion for guitars – and in his later years he had become quite a success story. While many other guitar makers seemed to live on a shoestring and never saw the financial fruits of their labor, D'Aquisto might be paid around $50,000 for a new archtop in the 1990s, an apparently unprecedented sum. He still loved nothing more than to talk guitars, but he was never critical of anybody else's work – to some extent he may even have been oblivious. Perhaps he realized, honestly and humbly, that he was the best at what he was doing.

▲ D'AQUISTO SOLO

PRODUCED: *c1990-1995*

THIS EXAMPLE: *Aug. 1992; serial 1238*

BODY: *17" wide, 3⅛" deep*

This is an astonishing example of D'Aquisto's work (back also shown, below left). It was commissioned by the late Scott Chinery, who named it his favorite D'Aquisto – and also his favorite guitar in the world. "I played it for ten hours straight as soon as I got it," said Chinery, "and only stopped because my fingers were bleeding. Then I woke at three in the morning and had to go play it some more. This guitar called out to me."

▲ D'AQUISTO AVANT-GARDE

PRODUCED: *1988-1995*

THIS EXAMPLE: *Sep. 1993; serial 1248*

BODY: *18" wide, 3⅛" deep*

By the time this appeared, D'Aquisto had peeled away superfluous decoration to get closer to the true heart of the archtop instrument. Binding was almost non-existent, soundholes were simple and elegant, and flourishes were limited to a refined peghead display. An apt name, too; it means "the leader in new or unconventional movements."

D'Aquisto, like many guitar makers working as a small, one-man operation, found that a good deal of his work was determined not so much by what he wanted to make and experiment with, but what his customers asked for. Many players ordered from D'Aquisto what they knew he made best: a top quality, traditional, acoustic archtop guitar. But during the last ten years of his life, thanks to some adventurous commissions, he began to push the idea of the archtop guitar beyond the traditional and into the future.

From the late 1980s D'Aquisto was changing and remodeling a number of key elements in his designs. Most apparent visually are new headstock and soundhole forms, and stylistic elements such as wooden tailpieces from earlier instruments were reaching fruition. Despite the keen visual

◀ D'AQUISTO CENTURA

PRODUCED: c1991-1995

THIS EXAMPLE: Aug. 1992; serial 1241

BODY: 17" wide, 3⅛" deep

The instruments here, which D'Aquisto called the "futuristic" group, are probably his most significant and important guitars. He struggled to break away from the traditional archtop design that he felt locked into – and this was the result. They have a more open sound than traditional archtops, and while the old-style guitars were primarily designed for rhythm in a jazz band, that might be the last style of music one would feel inclined to play on these modern, versatile D'Aquistos.

▼ D'AQUISTO ADVANCE

THIS EXAMPLE: Jun. 1994; serial 1255

BODY: 18" wide, 3¼" deep

D'Aquisto built a group of six guitars for collector Scott Chinery, and when it came to the last one the maker asked, "What do you want?" And the only direction Chinery gave him was quite simple. "Look into a crystal ball and show me what an archtop guitar is going to be like a hundred years from now," was Chinery's brief. D'Aquisto was always thinking so far ahead, but this was designed to make him go yet further. This unique guitar is what he came up with. The tailpiece adjusts to alter both the break-angle and length of the strings, and the soundholes have baffles that pop in and out to create tonal variations (it's shown here with the baffles in place).

▲ D'AQUISTO SOLO CUTAWAY

PRODUCED: c1990-1995

THIS EXAMPLE: Aug. 1992; serial 1239

BODY: 17" wide, 3⅛" deep

D'Aquisto spoke of a player who came to D'Angelico's shop and was always cold and arrogant toward him. Once he came in for a repair; D'Angelico said D'Aquisto would do it. The player made a remark, and D'Angelico blew up: "Get out of here! Some day he'll be making better guitars than me." And every time D'Aquisto told the story, he'd cry.

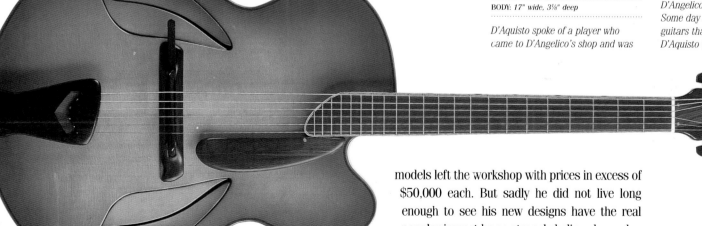

sense evident in these later instruments, the aim was, as ever, to create an object that worked musically. The newer guitars were designed for tonal purity and sound-projecting power, as well as a musical versatility that would take them beyond the limiting "jazz guitar" label so often applied to archtops. And D'Aquisto, unlike many luthiers, saw handsome rewards for his craftsmanship – a few of these new models left the workshop with prices in excess of $50,000 each. But sadly he did not live long enough to see his new designs have the real popular impact he so strongly believed was due to them. After D'Aquisto's untimely death in 1995, at the age of just 59, guitarist and D'Aquisto customer Steve Miller, best known for hits like 'Fly Like An Eagle,' wrote in *20th Century Guitar*: "I will try to honor and remember D'Aquisto by trying to play these instruments with as much love and kindness and soul as he put into them when he built them. He truly gave more than he received." And as D'Aquisto himself said of his guitars in Paul Schmidt's *Acquired Of The Angels*: "They are something I can leave behind and a way that I can make the world a bit better."

1968

MICRO-FRETS RELEASES THE
FIRST WIRELESS GUITAR

Amid a flurry of weird Sixties
ideas, the small Micro-Frets
company comes up with the
wireless guitar, which uses FM
radio waves rather than the
usual cord to connect the
instrument to its amplifier.

▶ **MOSRITE CUSTOM**

THIS EXAMPLE: *1980*

BODY: *15¼" wide, 2⅛" deep*

Semie Moseley made this guitar
(back shown left) in California and
gave it to his business partner of the
time, Robert Gentry, just before the
Mosrite company relocated to
Nevada. It's an astonishing example
of the guitar as work of art. Just
note the workmanship that went into
this instrument: beautiful timbers
and hand-cast hardware, as well as
highly ornate body carving and some
detailed marquetry.

◀ **MICRO-FRETS THE ORBITER**

PRODUCED: *c1968*

THIS EXAMPLE: *c1968; serial 1286*

BODY: *14¼" wide, 2" deep*

This was the model with which the
Maryland-based Micro-Frets
company introduced the idea of the
wireless guitar. An FM radio
transmitter was built into the guitar,
and the antenna can be seen here
projecting from the bass horn. An
off-stage receiver picked up the
signals and directed them to an
amplifier. In fact, The Orbiter was a
shortlived model – one variation has
an accentuated "second cutaway" on
the bass side, while another version
was called The Voyager. However, on
a pricelist from around 1970 Micro-
Frets was offering "our exclusive
patented FM Broadcasting System"
as an option on any of the
company's guitars or basses for an
extra $98.50. Micro-Frets lasted
from 1967 to about 1974, when it
was bought and moved to Virginia,
as Diamond-S, but only lasted a year
or two more before closing for good.

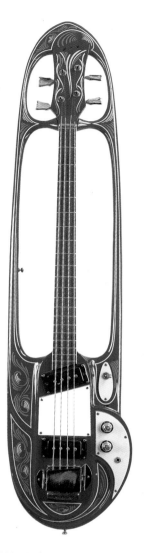

◄ MOSRITE "STRAWBERRY SIX" CUSTOM

THIS EXAMPLE: *1967*

BODY: *9½" wide, 1¼" deep*

Strawberry Alarm Clock was formed in California in 1967 and had a hit that year with a slice of psychedelia called, appropriately, 'Incense And Peppermints.' Rhythm guitarist Lee Freeman recalls: "Shortly after its release in May 1967, Semie Moseley gave us these three custom one-of-a-kind Mosrite guitars that he had personally hand-crafted for us. We performed live, in the studio and on TV with these three instruments during the peak of our popularity." The band had more hits with 'Sit With The Guru' and 'Tomorrow,' but split in 1971, and lead guitarist Ed King went off to join Lynyrd Skynyrd.

▲ MOSRITE "STRAWBERRY FOUR" CUSTOM

THIS EXAMPLE: *1967*

BODY: *10¾" wide, 1¼" deep*

Semie Moseley custom built the three unusual Mosrite electric lyre guitars shown here in 1967 for the psychedelic rock group, Strawberry Alarm Clock. This bass guitar would have been used by the band's first bass player, Gary Lovetro.

▲ MOSRITE "STRAWBERRY 12" CUSTOM

THIS EXAMPLE: *1967*

BODY: *10¼" wide, 1¼" deep*

This group of instruments was specially built for Strawberry Alarm Clock by Semie Moseley, founder of Mosrite. The painted decoration was added by California artist Von Dutch, well known in the hot-rod and custom-bike worlds of the time.

▲ RICKENBACKER 331 "LIGHT SHOW"

PRODUCED: *1970-1976*

THIS EXAMPLE: *Jul. 1971; serial KG446*

BODY: *14¾" wide, 2" deep*

Rickenbacker took the psychedelic light-show that was usually projected behind a band on stage and put it into a guitar. Devised by Stephen Woodman and Marshall Arm, it had an array of colored bulbs inside the body which flashed in response to the notes being played. But the model proved unpredictable due to over-heating, and has been likened to playing a toaster with pickups.

During the 1960s, as rock music became almost an international obsession, the American guitar industry saw a peak of sales in the wake of the guitar-fueled music – followed by a sharp decline at the end of the decade. During the peak, all manner of interesting and often strange designs were tried out, boosted by the prospect of potentially high sales for a guitar that might catch the popular, drug-soaked mood. For a few short years, just about anything seemed possible.

In Frederick, Maryland, a company called Micro-Frets and its founder Ralph Jones had their 15 minutes of fame by introducing the first wireless guitar, The Orbiter, in 1968. Today it's commonplace to see guitars and microphones linked from the live stage by wireless transmitters, but in '68 it was a wild new idea. Micro-Frets also used an unusual two-piece hollowed-out body construction for most of its guitars, as well as introducing the complex Calibrato vibrato system and the Micro-Nut, apparently designed for tuning stability and intonation improvement. Tom Wheeler summed up the company in his *American Guitars*: "Micro-Frets guitars were innovative if not particularly successful, and demonstrated a fierce commitment to space-age newness."

Semie Moseley was another dazzling if wayward designer, and his Mosrite operation, at first based in California, was most famous for its Ventures models of the 1960s, inspired by the instrumental group. Moseley had started building custom guitars in the 1950s for players such as Joe Maphis, and from the 1960s onwards would stop and then restart his business with alarming regularity. He died in 1992, at the age of 57.

▼ MARTIN D-45 CUSTOM

THIS EXAMPLE: *1983; serial 445105*

BODY: *15⅝" wide, 4⅞" deep*

As well as its *Guitar Of The Month* program of limited editions that began in 1984, Martin's custom shop has since its inception in 1979 produced special-order one-off items with appointments decided by the individual customer. This can result in beautiful examples such as this highly decorated D-45. Only a small number of original D-45s had been made by Martin before World War II (see p.53) and production of what must be one of the company's most revered instruments did not recommence until 1968.

1979

MARTIN ESTABLISHES CUSTOM SHOP

Ahead of the other major guitar manufacturers, Martin sets up a shop to produce custom orders and limited edition instruments.

▼ MARTIN D-45 NEIMAN MARCUS CUSTOM

THIS EXAMPLE: *1980; serial 424107*

BODY: *15½" wide, 4¾" deep*

The first Neiman Marcus store opened in Dallas, Texas, in 1907; by the 1990s there were 29 throughout the U.S. and the company described itself as a "fashion icon," with a reputation for top quality and

exclusive merchandise. In its 1980 Christmas mail-order catalog (cover, far left) Neiman Marcus included a one-off Martin D-45 built specially by the custom shop, described in the

> C.F. MARTIN NAZARETH, PA.
> EXCLUSIVE D-45 MADE FOR NEIMAN-MARCUS
> SERIAL NO. 424107

catalog (left) as an "unprecedented musical event." A plaque on the guitar case (inset) described the

guitar as "exclusive." The catalog noted the unique Martin's Brazilian rosewood back and sides, solid gold bridge pins and hand-inlaid abalone "tree-of-life" fingerboard decoration. The catalog entry closed with a nod to Martin's longevity: "With six generations of experience, this guitar may be their finest." The price of this one-off was $9,500, at a time when a regular D-45 listed for $2,820.

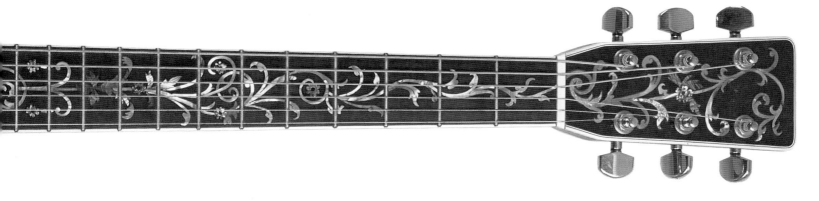

▼ MARTIN 7-45 CUSTOM

THIS EXAMPLE: *1981; serial 430755*

BODY: *13½" wide, 4¼" deep*

After a certain length of service with the company, Martin employees can make a personal instrument for themselves. This guitar was the

instrument that Dick Boak built. Boak had joined Martin in 1976 as a draftsman, and went on to head Martin's advertising department. The instrument is an exquisitely crafted Style 45 dreadnought, but with the smaller dimensions of size 7 (which had first appeared the previous year for the 7-28 and 7-37 models).

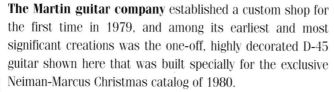

The Martin guitar company established a custom shop for the first time in 1979, and among its earliest and most significant creations was the one-off, highly decorated D-45 guitar shown here that was built specially for the exclusive Neiman-Marcus Christmas catalog of 1980.

A custom shop can mean different things to different guitar makers, but usually implies a separate workshop within the company that produces instruments apart from the normal production models. For example, these can be idiosyncratic creations built for imaginative customers, one-off guitars for important musicians, limited runs and editions of special models, or small personalized batches for individual retailers or retail chains. In effect, a custom shop is intended to enable a larger company to have some of the flexibility of the small

luthier, responsive to the individual whims of its customers. When Martin inaugurated its custom shop in 1979 it was one of the first major makers to do so, and was followed by companies such as Gibson (in 1983) and Fender (1987).

One of Martin's most successful marketing programs of recent years has been its custom shop's Guitar Of The Month scheme, which began in 1984. Despite the name, the program was soon modified from a guitar every month to the regular issue of around five limited edition instruments per year. They range in style from a recaptured vintage feel, such as 1984's 00-18V (one of the first), to an artist special such as the 1995 000-42EC that was based on Eric Clapton's 1939 000-42 used prominently on *Unplugged*, and produced in an almost instantly sold-out limited edition (see also p.126).

1995

MANZER BUILDS THE 42-STRING PIKASSO II

After producing an original instrument following a request by jazz guitarist Pat Metheny, Canadian guitar maker Linda Manzer crafts another artistic masterpiece that deploys 42 strings on four necks.

▼ **MANZER PIKASSO II**

THIS EXAMPLE: *1995; serial 10188*

BODY: *18¼″ wide, 4″ deep*

In 1986 Canadian guitar maker Linda Manzer was asked by acclaimed jazz guitarist Pat Metheny to build a guitar for him with "as many strings as possible." The result was the 42-string Pikasso, which had an on-board piezo pickup system. Collector Scott Chinery saw a picture of that in a magazine, and called up Linda to say how he'd love to have one. This strictly acoustic version was only the second Pikasso she's built. It came with a stand, either for show, or to leave your hands free for playing.

▲ SMITH 18-STRING

THIS EXAMPLE: *c1986; serial 2*

BODY: *16" wide, 4½" deep*

This amazing 18-string guitar was
built by another relatively obscure
maker, Ralph G. Smith of Wichita
(and Haysville), Kansas. Smith made

at least three more flat-tops in this
style. The instrument takes the
12-string concept a step further by
adopting six three-string courses,
and produces a mighty sound as a
result. The necessarily extra-long
peghead, extended to incorporate
the nine-a-side tuning machines,
does make the guitar head-heavy.

▼ BARKER SEVEN-STRING

THIS EXAMPLE: *1985; serial 7985*

BODY: *18" wide, 3¼" deep*

This attractive archtop instrument
was built by maker William Barker,
who previously worked
for Albanus (see

far right). At one time he was based
in Bartonville, near Peoria, Illinois.
Barker did make regular six-string
guitars, but this unusual seven-
string is a far more intriguing
instrument. As with most seven-
string guitars, the additional low-
pitched string is designed to be
tuned below the low E.

Six strings are without doubt the standard complement for
guitars today, but instrument makers and musicians have
constantly toyed with the potential for more, either as
additional individual strings, or extra doubled and even
tripled sets, known as "courses."

The best-known variant of the standard six-string guitar is
the 12-string guitar (see, for example, the Stella 12-string on
p.51) where the original six strings are doubled into paired
"courses," creating a wonderfully thick, jangling tone that
sounds something like two guitars playing together.

In fact, for the first few hundred years of its life, the early
guitar in Europe had been made for four, five, and then six
courses of strings – in other words, eight-string, ten-string
and 12-string guitars. The move to the "modern" complement

▲ D'AQUISTO CENTURA DELUXE

THIS EXAMPLE: *Apr. 1994; serial 1252*

BODY: *18″ wide, 1⅛″ deep*

Scott Chinery chose the Centura Deluxe as the basis for his Blue Guitar collection: the specifications he gave to the 21 other makers were based on this fine instrument, which he considered one of the most amazing guitars ever made. It's a tremendously versatile instrument: one moment sweet like a flat-top, another roaring like a Stromberg. D'Aquisto was trying to expand the horizons of the archtop guitar, and many of his "modern" guitars possess this wonderful versatility.

The idea for the Blue Guitar Collection came to the late guitar-collector Scott Chinery who wanted to celebrate the regeneration during recent years of the art of the archtop guitar. He considered the luthiers of our time to be producing the finest instruments of their kind ever made, so he set 21 builders to work, interpreting the 18″-wide cutaway archtop guitar in a set of related instruments.

One of Chinery's few specifications was that the guitars be finished in blue. This unusual choice was inspired by his 1994 D'Aquisto Centura Deluxe. Chinery knew that D'Aquisto had to be part of this historic collection, and since D'Aquisto had already died when the idea was conceived, he chose one of the great guitar-maker's instruments to form the basis of the project. Chinery said, "I tried to pick 21 guitar makers – in

addition to the inspirational D'Aquisto – whose work would be individually distinctive from one another. I wanted to have the whole breadth of experience and of price represented: the new Blue Guitars cost from $3,500 to $35,000 each."

Pictured on these pages are six selected guitars from the Blue Collection, made by Benedetto, Bozo, Campellone, Collings, D'Aquisto, and Monteleone. The other 16 were made by Buscarino, Comins, D'Leco, Fender, Gibson, Grimes, Hollenback, Lacey, Manzer, Megas, Nickerson, Ribbecke, Scharpach, Triggs, Walker, and Zeidler.

These makers are from a variety of backgrounds, reflecting the diversity of experience behind contemporary guitars. For example, Mark Campellone was a musician first, his guitar-making skills largely self taught, although an ex-Guild

1996

BLUE GUITAR COLLECTION
SHOWCASES ARCHTOPS

*Collector Scott Chinery
commissions 21 makers to build
the Blue Guitar Collection, based
on his D'Aquisto Centura Deluxe.*

▲ **COLLINGS CUSTOM**

THIS EXAMPLE: *1996*

BODY: *18" wide, 3¼" deep*

*Bill Collings has been one of the pre-
eminent instrument builders to have
emerged during the past 20 years.
He is currently based in Austin,
Texas – and some who have played
this guitar feel that it has a sound
almost as big as Texas! Although
Collings's production of archtop
guitars has in recent years*
*diminished in favor of flat-top
instruments, this example proves
that he certainly has not forgotte[n]
how to carve out a great jazz box.
Players report it a dream to play,
a number of the design elements
appealing too, not least the rand[om]
"flying chip" inlays on the neck a[nd]
the headstock, which seem some[how]
to add to the guitar's intelligent
approach. The intense blue color [is]
quite stunning, even when seen
among so many other instrumen[ts of]
a broadly similar hue.*

► ALBANUS SEVEN-STRING

THIS EXAMPLE: *c1954*

BODY: *18" wide, 3¼" deep*

*Among some of the more obscure
makers whose work is in this book,
Albanus is probably the least well
known. Another low-A seven-
stringer, this is labeled "Carl Albanus
Johnson, Chicago." Johnson was still
working in Chicago as late as 1976.*

▲ KOONTZ 17-7

THIS EXAMPLE: *May 1978; serial 3*

BODY: *17" wide, 3¼" deep*

*Sam Koontz of Linden, New Jersey,
is noted for unusual and high
quality work, and this seven-string
guitar with an oval soundhole is a
fine example of his craftsmanship.*

single strings was made only relatively recently, around
, and the six-string guitar was quickly established as the
mark throughout Europe and also in America.

ore recently, some players have opted for an increase of
ower-tuned string, resulting in the seven-string guitar,
several examples are shown here. One of the earliest
rs to use such an instrument was George Van Eps,
rist with Ray Noble and Benny Goodman in the 1930s,
moved to California in 1936 and shortly afterwards had
one build him his special seven-string guitar. He later
ribed this as "a complete instrument within itself," a
nce to the extended bass range afforded by the extra
string. A production version of Van Eps' seven-string
ade by Gretsch from 1968 and stayed in its catalog for

around ten years, while a later version of the idea was Steve
Vai's recent solidbody seven-string for Ibanez.

The Manzer 42-string Pikasso guitar is something else
altogether. The instrument does actually center on a standard
six-string neck; parallel to that is a very short, additional,
unfretted 12-string "neck" as one might find on a harp guitar,
and then two further sets of sympathetic strings, one as
another 12-string "neck," as well as a two-way 12-string body
extension. Manzer has only made two of these astonishing 42-
string instruments: the Pikasso II, commissioned by collector
Scott Chinery Collection (pictured far left), and the original
Pikasso built specially for jazz guitarist Pat Metheny, who told
Guitar Player in 1992: "[It] can do some far-out things. I'd like
to take a year off just to discover its full potential."

◀ BOZO CHICAGOAN

THIS EXAMPLE: *Feb. 1996; serial 501-4*

BODY: *18" wide, 3⅜" deep*

Bozo Podunavac is a master of the art of inlay, as exemplified on this impressive instrument. His guitars are instantly recognizable by their trademark peghead, as well as the herringbone and abalone purfling. The Chicagoan, named for Bozo's adopted home after he immigrated in the 1950s, has a powerful tone and a great sound. The intricacy of the tailpiece engraving and the majestic fingerboard are graceful testaments to this refined maker. He is now based in Florida, and still makes instruments.

▲ BENEDETTO LA CREMONA AZZURA

THIS EXAMPLE: *1996; serial 37996*

BODY: *18" wide, 3" deep*

This turned out to be the loudest instrument in the Blue Guitar Collection, and many players who have encountered it report it to be among the loudest they've heard. But there's more than just power

here: at times it is almost organ-like or piano-like. The openings on the upper bout are an interesting design feature, aiming to bring the player closer to the pure sound. The late Scott Chinery, who commissioned the Blue Guitar Collection, said: "I feel that if Michelangelo has an equivalent in the art of luthiery, it is Bob Benedetto; and if Michelangelo's Pieta sculpture has an equivalent, it is Benedetto's La Cremona Azzurra."

▲ CAMPELLONE SPECIAL

THIS EXAMPLE: *1995; serial 720995*

BODY: *18" wide, 3½" deep*

This was made by Mark Campellone in Providence, Rhode Island, and it has strong ties to traditional archtop design. The sheer physical presence of this Campellone is notable: that abalone fleur-de-lis on the pickguard almost seems to jump off the instrument as you look at it.

▲ MONTELEONE ROCKET CONVERTIBLE

THIS EXAMPLE: *Oct. 1995; serial 166*

BODY: *18" wide, 3" deep*

John Monteleone builds his guitars in Islip, New York. This guitar has tone-altering "side-ports", as suggested by Chinery. They can be partly or totally closed by moving a handled "door" across the aperture. In addition, the knob by the neck operates a cover which slides across the elegant front soundhole (shown totally closed in the main picture).

craftsman helped with general guidelines on archtop construction. Bozo Podunavac, meanwhile, had started out in his native Yugoslavia in the early 1950s, apprenticed to luthier Milutin Mladenovich in Belgrade, emigrating to Chicago in 1959. Mark Lacey did a three-year full-time Musical Instrument Technology course at the London College of Furniture before working in Norway and then around America, finally opening his own workshop in Los Angeles during 1988.

And for Linda Manzer a hobby in the late 1960s progressed to an apprenticeship with fellow Canadian Jean Larrivee in the 1970s, plus a later term of study with Jimmy D'Aquisto. So where do budding young guitar-makers go for help now? Manzer: "For anyone interested in luthiery, I recommend

joining the Association of Stringed Instrument Artisans (A.S.I.A.) as well as reading their magazine *Guitarmaker*. Also, there are many great books available that are a wonderful first step. If you have a dream, follow it. I did."

Bob Benedetto told *Acoustic Guitar* magazine in 1994, "Sound is subjective. I would have to say that the truly handmade archtops produced by today's luthiers – and there really aren't that many of us – are every bit as good and in some cases better than the older D'Angelicos, Epiphones and Gibsons. But this is only because we have continued where the older makers left off," Benedetto emphasized. "If one person makes enough guitars, he or she will begin to develop a personal, distinctive sound. I'm not sure if it's planned that way: we simply learn by doing."

▼ CARVIN ALLAN HOLDSWORTH

PRODUCED: *1996-current*

THIS EXAMPLE: *1997*

BODY: *12" wide, 1 ¾" deep*

Carvin began in the 1940s primarily as an amp maker, but added guitars to its lines during the following decade. Endorsers of the company's more recent solidbody guitars have included Jason Becker of the David Lee Roth band and jazz guitarist Al DiMeola, but the launch of the Allan Holdsworth model aligned Carvin with a remarkably talented English fretman.

1996

PEAVEY ISSUES EDDIE VAN HALEN SIGNATURE MODEL

"Signature" guitars, endorsed by famous players, date back at least to Gibson's Nick Lucas model of 1928 (see p.40), but in more recent decades the practice is mushrooming.

Guitar companies have for a long time seen the value of enticing top players to use their instruments. Sometimes, of course, no enticement is necessary, and the player just happens to be using a brand of guitar out of personal choice. The company simply moves in to make such an arrangement official. Otherwise the guitar manufacturer has to persuade a player to use a particular instrument, either through innovation or other temptation. In each situation, the company generally offers services to the touring player and, usually, some kind of financial deal, in exchange for using the player's name and/or image in promotion for the "signature" model in question.

It is not difficult to think of early examples of this kind of activity. It's generally accepted that the first instance of the so-called "signature guitar" for an American company resulted in the launch of Gibson's Nick Lucas model in the late 1920s – and more detail on this story has already been covered in these pages (see p.40-41).

Probably the next well-known example of the signature guitar also came from Gibson, with the Les Paul solidbody model, which first came on to the market in the early 1950s. This set the trend for an enormous number of meetings of acoustic and electric guitars with guitar stars over the coming years, and some of the more recent examples are presented here, on these and the following pages.

Many more "signatures" are or have been in evidence in the guitar industry: PRS with Carlos Santana; Brian Setzer with Gretsch; Taylor with Richie Sambora; Eddie Van Halen with

► **PEAVEY T-60**

PRODUCED: *1978-1989*

THIS EXAMPLE: *1979*

BODY: *12 ½" wide, 1 ½" deep*

Peavey, founded in Mississippi by Hartley Peavey in the 1960s, is best known for amps, but this model was the first of a long line of guitars.

◄ **PEAVEY EVH WOLFGANG**

PRODUCED: *1996-current*

THIS EXAMPLE: *1997*

BODY: *13" wide, 1 ⅞" deep*

Eddie Van Halen moved allegiance from the Music Man company to Peavey in the mid 1990s resulting in a new series of solidbody electrics. Van Halen had already worked with Peavey on some amplifiers. The new guitars featured a double-cutaway body, and a full-travel double-locking tremolo system, as seen on the example pictured here and so much associated with Van Halen's demonstrative playing style.

▲ **WASHBURN PAUL STANLEY PS-500**

PRODUCED: *1998-2000*

THIS EXAMPLE: *1999*

BODY: *13" wide, 1 ½" deep*

The history of the earlier years of the Washburn brand has been covered elsewhere in this book, but more recently its instruments have been manufactured in the Far East as well as some still made in the US. This model was produced to mark an arrangement with the Kiss guitarist, and brings to mind the shape of the Ibanez Iceman with which the white-faced fret-demon was associated in the band's heyday.

▼ **RICKENBACKER 1998PT PETE TOWNSHEND**

PRODUCED: *1987-88*

THIS EXAMPLE: *Aug. 1988*

BODY: *15" wide, 2" deep*

Rickenbacker produced the world's first commercial electric guitar with a magnetic pickup in the early 1930s, but is best known for distinctive designs that date back to the 1950s and their use in the 1960s by The Beatles and The Byrds. Another prime Rick user – and abuser – was The Who's Pete Townshend, honored in 1987 with this limited-edition signature model.

► **GIBSON JOE PERRY**

PRODUCED: *1996-current*

THIS EXAMPLE: *1997*

BODY: *12¾" wide, 2" deep*

Gibson's revered Les Paul models have attracted a greater number of well known players than any other of the company's electric models, and thus have been the target for many "signature" offerings. This one began life in the late 1990s after collaboration with the guitarist from Aerosmith, a band now apparently immovable from the stadium circuit.

Kramer and Music Man before he linked up with Peavey; Rickenbacker with Tom Petty; Martin with Gene Autry. There was a time, most notably during the 1970s and 1980s, when the lesser cousin of the signature guitar, the "endorsement deal," began to acquire a negative aura. The endorsement deal is simply where a player appears in ads saying that he or she uses a particular instrument. No signature guitar is produced; the musician just "endorses" the brand and/or model by association.

The core problem that developed in those earlier decades involved trust, mainly because of players who would happily endorse a brand and take the money ... without ever playing the guitar in question. Audiences would notice that player X,

who would be seen in all the guitar magazines cheerfully promoting the advantages of brand Y, was clearly appearing on stage night after night still playing the same old brand Z that they'd be using for years. It is much less prevalent today, and it seems that both musicians and manufacturers have become more honest about the whole arrangement – sensing, no doubt, that no one is going to fooled for too long if there is deception, and that nobody gains in the long term from what effectively amounts to false information.

Signature models too are launched these days with a stronger understanding of musical worth and commercial reality. Nonetheless, in extreme cases there is sometimes the sense that the oddities of one player's technical requirements will not necessarily suit a great number of other musicians.

▲ **MARTIN 000-42ECB CLAPTON**

PRODUCED: *2000-2001*

THIS EXAMPLE: *2000*

BODY: *15⅛" wide, 4" deep*

Martin first issued a Clapton signature model, the 000-42EC, in 1995. The edition of 461 (recalling Clapton's 461 Ocean Boulevard album) sold out within days. There followed a "stock" model, still on sale and so far up to about 4,000 sales. Only 200 of this new limited hand-signed ECB edition were made, using ultimate materials that included rare Brazilian rosewood from Martin's small supply of certified timber.

▼ FENDER JIMI HENDRIX STRAT

PRODUCED: *1997-2000*

THIS EXAMPLE: *1997*

BODY: *12¼" wide, 1" deep*

Here's a weird one – concentrate, now. Jimi was a left-hander, of course, but the majority of potential customers for a signature model will, figured Fender, be right-handed. So the company made a completely reversed version of one of Jimi's typical late-1960s Strats. Jimi, you will recall, used a regular right-handed Strat "upside down". So this signature edition is, in effect, a left-handed model turned upside down and re-strung, thus recreating Jimi's experience in reverse. Got it? A final flourish from an evidently flustered Fender was to add the normal headstock logo in reverse, so that the adoring new owner can look at themselves in the mirror with the

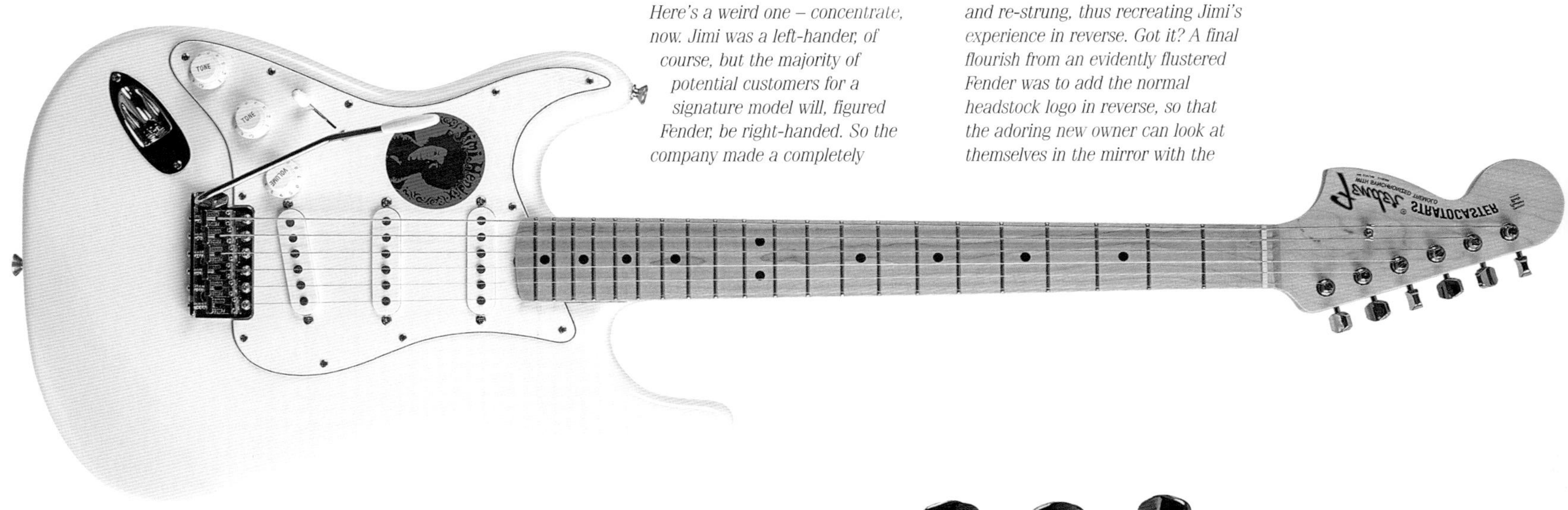

► EPIPHONE NOEL GALLAGHER

PRODUCED: *1997-current*

THIS EXAMPLE: *1998*

BODY: *15¾" wide, 1¾" deep*

This Supernova is the more tasteful of the two signature models produced to celebrate the use of Epiphone Sheraton guitars by the Oasis guitarist. Its companion matches the look of Gallagher's original, boasting a bold British Union flag covering the body, and widely seen as symbolizing the great surge of "Britpop" bands which reached the dizziest heights of musical re-invention in the 1990s.

▼ TAYLOR LKSM-6 LEO KOTTKE

PRODUCED: *1996-current*

THIS EXAMPLE: *1997*

BODY: *17" wide, 4¼" deep*

Taylor first launched a signature guitar for the great Kottke in 1990, a 12-string model known as the LKSM, this six-string version following later in the decade. Kottke was drawn to Taylor's design clarity, to the guitar's fine sound, and to the utility of a production instrument that could be easily repaired: "A practical instrument," he says.

▶ **PARKER MIDI FLY**

PRODUCED: *1999-current*

THIS EXAMPLE: *1999*

BODY: *12" wide, 1" deep*

This is Parker's take on the "synth access" guitar, an instrument with built-in MIDI facilities that allow the player to use a wide range of sounds from a remote synthesizer unit.

▲ **PARKER FLY ARTIST**

PRODUCED: *1997-current*

THIS EXAMPLE: *1997*

BODY: *12" wide, 1" deep*

Parker is a partnership between guitar-maker Ken Parker and electronics expert Larry Fishman. Financed by Korg, the operation began

producing instruments in 1993, based near Boston, Massachusetts. The company's Fly models employ a radical new construction method that features extra-thin, lightweight wooden bodies strengthened by a composite carbon/epoxy material forming a thin "external skeleton" around the wood. Necks are similarly made, while sounds are generally combined from "acoustic" piezo pickups and conventional magnetic "electric" units.

1997

DEVELOPMENT OF THE
ACOUSTIC-ELECTRIC HYBRID

Parker launches the latest in its Fly series of "hybrid" models, the spruce-and-composite Fly Artist.

▶ **GIBSON CHET ATKINS CEC**

PRODUCED: *1982-current*

THIS EXAMPLE: *1990;*

BODY: *13¼" wide, 1⅝" deep*

This collaboration between Gibson and ace guitarist Chet Atkins provided a practical electric classical guitar. At last it was possible for players to achieve a convincing amplified nylon-string sound from an instrument that played and felt like a well-appointed classical guitar, thanks to the application of piezo-style pickup technology.

▲ HAMER DUO TONE

PRODUCED: *1993-current*

THIS EXAMPLE: *1994*

BODY: *12 ½" wide, 1 ¾" deep*

Hamer was founded by Paul Hamer and Jol Dantzig in Illinois in the mid 1970s, making respected Gibson-inspired models. In 1988 Hamer was acquired by Ovation's owners, Kaman. A 1990s introduction by the new firm was the Duo Tone model, a "hybrid" that combines electric and acoustic sounds.

▼ OVATION CUSTOM LEGEND 1619

PRODUCED: *1974-1996*

THIS EXAMPLE: *1976*

BODY: *13 ½" wide, 3" deep*

Ovation was set up by aeronautical engineer Charles H. Kaman in Bloomfield, Connecticut, in 1966.

The brand's revolutionary "Lyrachord" bowl-back acoustics were soon made even more exciting by the addition of bridge-mounted under-saddle "piezo" pickups, with side-mounted controls as seen on this Custom Legend. A great number of related models have followed, including the impressive multi-soundhole Adamas line.

▼ GODIN LG-XT

PRODUCED: *1998-current*

THIS EXAMPLE: *1998*

BODY: *12" wide, 1 ½" deep*

Located in Canada, Godin was established by Robert Godin in the early 1980s. Several innovative models have appeared from the maker, including 1993's Multiac "synth access" model for easy links to a synthesizer, and this later LG-XT with its piezo-equipped "X-bridge".

Magnetic pickups have defined the sound of electric guitars since the earliest experiments of the 1930s, but it wasn't until Ovation produced a viable "piezo" pickup mounted in a guitar's bridge in the late 1960s that the idea of an "acoustic electric" sound began to develop. A piezo pickup employs piezo-electric crystals which generate an electrical signal when those crystals experience what technicians term "mechanical strain" and we would call movement.

In a guitar, the movement sensed is in the strings and in the body – and primarily the top of the body. Because the piezo pickup senses movement in this way it produces a tone that is more closely allied to the instrument's acoustic sound, as opposed to the "pure electric" sound of a conventional magnetic pickup. At first Ovation had much of the business of electric-acoustic guitars to itself. Gradually musicians began to appreciate the value of a guitar that could produce a reasonably authentic amplified acoustic sound, especially on-stage. Such guitars became known as electro-acoustics, or just plain electros.

Today, the application of piezo pickups has spread to a new kind of "hybrid" guitar which combines the familiar sound of electric magnetic pickups with the more acoustic-sounding tones of piezos. One of the companies which has worked toward a practical combination is Parker, whose Fly series also uses radical new construction methods. A number of other proponents of piezo pickups and hybrids are also revealed in the instruments shown on these pages.

1998

PRS LAUNCHES ITS FIRST HOLLOWBODY MODELS

After years of quality service to players of solidbody electrics, PRS puts some air in its bodies.

◀ **PAUL REED SMITH'S FIRST GUITAR**

THIS EXAMPLE: *1975*

BODY: *12 ½" wide, 2" deep*

An early piece of work by the then-amateur guitar maker Paul Reed Smith, ten years before he set up the PRS operation. It reveals his early passion for Gibson double-cutaway Les Paul models, especially the two-pickup Special. The guitar was made while Smith was studying at his local college, and he received credits for the work. Such official encouragement at an early stage is crucial for the budding guitar maker.

◀ **PRS McCARTY HOLLOWBODY II**

PRODUCED: *1998-current*

THIS EXAMPLE: *1998*

BODY: *12 ½" wide, 1¾" deep*

This and the Archtop formed PRS's first stab at the hollowbody guitar market, and a very successful move it turned out to be. By the end of the launch year, hollowbodies accounted for half the company's output.

▲ **GUITAR FOR PETER FRAMPTON**

THIS EXAMPLE: *1976*

BODY: *13" wide, 2" deep*

Paul Reed Smith had by now set up as a guitar maker, and through sheer determination had a good deal of success in making guitars for relatively well known players. This is a good example, made for the then highly successful Frampton. Other recipients of early Smith instruments included Al DiMeola, Ted Nugent, and Howard Leese of Heart.

Paul Reed Smith had a simple idea: merge some of the best features of the two finest solidbody electric guitar makers – Gibson and Fender – and you could have a world-beating combination. A simple idea was all very well, but the way in which it was executed would ultimately determine its success. As it turned out, the PRS guitars produced since Smith formed his company in 1985 are testament to a determination and an attention to detail that few can match. Smith had worked as a freelance repairman and custom instrument maker for the previous ten years around Annapolis, Maryland, building successful instruments for influential players such

▶ **GUITAR FOR CARLOS SANTANA**

THIS EXAMPLE: *1980*

BODY: *12 ½" wide, 2" deep*

The most important guitar that Smith made in his "pre-factory" days, this is the first instrument he produced for Carlos Santana – and only the third maple-top guitar he'd built. Smith would make a number of other instruments for Santana in an association that continues to this day. The modern PRS company offers several Santana "signature" models.

▲ **PRS CUSTOM**

PRODUCED: *1985-current*

THIS EXAMPLE: *1985*

BODY: *12 ½" wide, 2" deep*

Smith and his partners set up PRS in 1985, and this was the second ever guitar to roll off the production lines. The Custom model continued Smith's fascination with maple tops.

▲ **DOUBLE-NECK GUITAR**

THIS EXAMPLE: *c1980*

BODY: *17" wide, 2 ¼" deep*

This impressive double-neck guitar was the "apprentice piece" made by Paul Reed Smith's faithful assistant John Ingram. The fledgling guitar-making operation was having trouble making enough money, although this instrument was sold to ex-Santana guitarist Neal Schon, who had earlier bought a six-string from Smith.

as Peter Frampton and, of greatest importance to future success, Carlos Santana. The first PRS model was the Custom, launched with the company in 1985 and embodying that evolutionary idea of combining Fender and Gibson-like elements. It had a double-cutaway body that melded Smith's original influence, Gibson's Les Paul Special, with the curviness of a Fender Stratocaster. The scale-length was half-way between Fender and Gibson's regular lengths, and an on-board mix control drew rich Gibson-like sounds and thinner Fender-style tones from two humbucking pickups.

Noting the 1980s fashion for complicated locking vibrato systems, Smith designed with an engineer a simple, practical vibrato system that updated the classic Fender unit. To cap it all, Smith's work recalled the great sunburst Les Paul

Standards of the late 1950s by employing beautifully figured maple tops. At the same time as the Custom, PRS also launched its Standard model, with an all-mahogany body rather than the mahogany/maple sandwich of the Custom. For many years PRS developed and refined this pair of models, adding variants and offspring, and growing gradually and effectively. PRS instruments have until recently always been expensive, so it was a significant development in 1987 when the Signature model was launched, effectively an even more opulent PRS. The Signature was a Custom, but this time made with even finer materials, notably some stunning figured timbers.

Supreme playability was becoming a matter of course for PRS guitars, but the Signature made it apparent to the

▶ **PRS CUSTOM 22 SOAPBAR**

PRODUCED: *1998-current*

THIS EXAMPLE: *1999*

BODY: *12 ½" wide, 2" deep*

The Custom 22 Soapbar is a typical PRS mix of Fender and Gibson influences that creates something new. Here was the first PRS model with a Fender-like complement of three pickups – although the units themselves recall Gibson's P-90 pickups.

▶ **PRS PRIVATE STOCK #62**

THIS EXAMPLE: *1998*

BODY: *12½" wide, 1¾" deep*

Private Stock guitars are custom-shop models that use the highest quality timbers available – and from a company that already has a high reputation for good wood. As this instrument shows, the results can be astonishing examples of the modern guitar-maker's art. Private Stock number 62 uses eastern red maple for its top, back (right) and sides, finished in PRS's violin amber color. The guitar features PRS's distinctive "bird" inlays on the fingerboard – though in keeping with this instrument's special status, the birds here are made of mammoth ivory with gold outlines.

▲ **PRS CUSTOM 22**

PRODUCED: *1993-current*

THIS EXAMPLE: *1994*

BODY: *12 ½" wide, 2" deep*

Here was the first major change to the prime PRS model, the Custom. Launched in 1993, the Custom 22 was effectively a production version of the ornate and expensive Dragon guitar of the previous year. The major and most obvious change was a move from 24 to 22 frets.

company's management team that there was a market for "ultimate" instruments in parallel to the already high-quality lines. Another guitar in this category was the Limited Edition, the first PRS with a non-vibrato bridge. The other end of the market called for a new model too, and the Classic Electric or CE was born, tipping the balance toward a Fender style with its alder body and bolt-on maple neck, and the EG, without PRS's notable carved top.

The Dragon of 1992 was festooned with a facsimile of Smith's favorite fire-breathing beast. Just 50 were created, but some sonic changes heralded a subtle but significant shift of gears for the PRS sound. These changes would reach most players in the form of the Custom 22

◄ PRS DRAGON 2000

PRODUCED: *1999-2000*

THIS EXAMPLE: *1999 prototype*

BODY: *12 ½" wide, 2" deep*

The high-end Dragon series began with a limited edition of 50 guitars in 1992, the Dragon I. Two more editions followed, the II and III in 1993 and 1994. The over-the-top Dragon 2000 employed a unique computer-cut three-dimensional inlay on the body that featured a host of different colored shells.

◄ PRS McCARTY SOAPBAR

PRODUCED: *1998-current*

THIS EXAMPLE: *1999*

BODY: *12 ½" wide, 2" deep*

Along with the Custom, PRS's McCarty solidbody models have been among the most successful for the Maryland guitar maker. This all-mahogany version with "soapbar" single-coils was a reaction to the fashionable interest in P-90-style pickups during the late 1990s.

▲ PRS SINGLECUT

PRODUCED: *2000-current*

THIS EXAMPLE: *2001*

BODY: *12 ½" wide, 2" deep*

"Over the years many companies have either blatantly copied the Les Paul or used it as clear inspiration," wrote Dave Burrluck, author of The PRS Guitar Book. "Yet the PRS Singlecut will be seen by many as the closest anyone has come to the hallowed tone of Gibson's late-1950s Les Paul without actually breaching any trademarked design features."

model, launched the following year. This 22-fret reworking of the classic Custom was in essence a Dragon without the expensive inlay work. In 1994 Smith's association with ex-Gibson chief Ted McCarty became public with the launch of the McCarty Model, this time tipping toward the Gibson camp and in particular the hallowed 1950s Les Paul models. PRS also began producing a Santana model a year after the McCarty first appeared, reflecting the early-style design that Smith had made for Santana in his pre-factory days as a custom builder.

An important new development for PRS came in 1998 when a new line of hollowbody models was launched, arriving as the McCarty Hollowbody and the extra-deep McCarty Archtop. The company's new computer-aided production machinery assisted in the detailed carving necessary to create the relatively complex internal structure of these new solid-wood models, and a new sound was made available from a PRS-brand guitar.

The new PRS Singlecut was launched in 2000 with ads that said: "Ted McCarty introduced the single cutaway, carved-top solidbody to the world in 1952. We learned a lot from Ted while we were working on ours." McCarty died in 2001.

The following year PRS launched its first non-U.S.-made guitar. The Santana SE was the company's most affordable guitar yet, putting the PRS brand within reach of middle-market buyers. And today, in terms of U.S. sales, PRS are pitched at number three behind their illustrious original inspirations, Fender and Gibson.

1999

DANELECTRO RELEASES RETRO U-3 MODEL

The reactivated Danelectro operation goes retro crazy with an eye-popping line of 50s and 60s-style designs.

◄ **B.C. RICH BICH NJ**

PRODUCED: *1998-current*

THIS EXAMPLE: *1999*

BODY: *13" wide, 1 ¼" deep*

B.C. Rich founder Bernardo Rico defined the outlandish guitar shape of the 1970s and 1980s, and a revitalized company has continued this particular art since 1994.

▶ **DANELECTRO STANDARD 3021**

PRODUCED: *1959-c1966*

THIS EXAMPLE: *1965*

BODY: *11 ½" wide, 1 ¼" deep*

One of the simply stylish Danelectro models from the 1950s upon which the brand's reputation stands, the Standard is best known for having been played by Led Zeppelin's guitarist Jimmy Page, primarily on-stage where he exploited its cutting sound for slide-guitar work. Years later the Danelectro brand reappeared on a new 1990s line.

▲ **DANELECTRO U-3**

PRODUCED: *1998-current*

THIS EXAMPLE: *1999*

BODY: *12" wide, 1 ½" deep*

Retro flavors were everywhere in the electric guitar world during the 1990s, and none more so than in the revived Danelectro brand, acquired by Evets in 1995. The original Danelectro U series had appeared in 1956, sold as the single-pickup U-1, the twin-pickup U-2 and, the following year, the triple-pickup U-3. The new company exploited the retro vibe, but added many of the benefits of modern construction.

▲ JACKSON SURFCASTER

PRODUCED: *1998-current*

THIS EXAMPLE: *1998*

BODY: *12 ½" wide, 1 ¾" deep*

One of the first signs of the impending retro fashion came in 1991 when the Jackson-related Charvel brand introduced the Surfcaster, a heady mix of design

influences from the 1950s – including "lipstick" pickups that recalled Danelectro, and Rickenbacker-style soundhole and fingerboard-inlays. The parent company, Jackson, also offered the model. Many other offshore as well as US-based companies took note of this early indication that retro could not only look good but also sound good – and sell well.

▼ JACKSON SOLOIST

PRODUCED: *c1983-1987*

THIS EXAMPLE: *1985*

BODY: *12" wide, 1 ¼" deep*

Jackson had made its own mark on the US guitar scene by developing the "superstrat" with its Soloist and other models, helping to define the look of 1980s rock guitars.

◄ DANELECTRO LONG HORN 4623

PRODUCED: *1958-1969*

THIS EXAMPLE: *1958*

BODY: *13" wide, 1 ¼" deep*

The Long Horn guitars are further examples of vintage Danelectros with a distinctive look that informed the style of retro instruments.

If there was one word that defined the electric guitar industry during the 1990s it was retro. Toward the end of the decade more guitar makers than ever were busily looking back to the past in a search for fresh inspiration, as the craze for retro flavors seemed to be everywhere.

It is easy enough to understand the trend. Some makers felt that there was almost no more to be done to the electric guitar, that it had reached its ultimate incarnation and that its general design, construction and manufacturing processes were just about as perfect as they could get.

So instead of going forwards, why not dredge up the best factors that made past instruments so distinctive, and catch a bonus from the fashionable retro vibe? This was a grand theory, but in some ways proved more difficult to put into

practice. Getting too close to those atmospheric looks of the great guitars of the 1950s, the 1960s, even the 1970s, could have expensive consequences if influence turned into stealing. Some companies solved the problem by buying an old name and re-establishing its retro look.

Probably the most successful take on this idea was Danelectro, credited by many as popularizing the whole retro electric guitar movement. Danelectro had been started in New York by Nat Daniel around 1946, at first to produce amps. But a series of cheaply-made, great sounding and cool looking instruments followed. However, MCA bought the operation, and closed it in 1969. Daniel died in 1994, and the following year Evets bought the Danelectro name and introduced some glorious retro guitars, starting in 1998.

1999

TAYLOR GUITARS CELEBRATES
TWENTY-FIFTH ANNIVERSARY

The major new success story in acoustic guitars is Taylor, based in California and gaining a growing reputation for keen style and rich playability.

◄ **TAYLOR 25th ANNIVERSARY**

PRODUCED: *1999*

THIS EXAMPLE: *1999*

BODY: *15⅞" wide, 4⅝" deep*

Only 500 of this special limited edition instrument were issued by Taylor in 1999 to celebrate the company's 25th year of operation. The business was begun in California in 1974 by Bob Taylor and Kurt Lustig and, like many new guitar-making operations, they experienced a shaky start. "Those early years were nothing but day after day of bad news," Bob Taylor recalled recently. "But we're a better, more resilient company now because of it."

◄ **TAYLOR PALLET GUITAR**

PRODUCED: *2000*

THIS EXAMPLE: *2000*

BODY: *15⅞" wide, 4¼" deep*

Bob Taylor made his original Pallet guitar in 1995 from scrap wood to prove that it's the guitar-maker's skill rather than materials which determine the quality of an instrument. But an experiment turned into orders – and so a limited edition of 25 more was made during 2000, also using "pallet-grade" oak, and now with a suitable fingerboard inlay of a forklift truck.

The history of the American guitar revealed in this book shows a marked continuity in one particular type of instrument: the flat-top acoustic. If you turn back to the opening pages, you'll find yourself in the 1830s, and among completely recognizable acoustic guitars, with waisted bodies, round soundholes, pin bridges, and raised fingerboards. And you don't have to turn forward much before a more familiar style of headstock emerges. So what has happened to the modern flat-top? Is it, today, simply an old design built with the benefits of modern construction?

Some of the answers will be revealed by the selection of contemporary acoustics shown on these and the following pages. Martin, who made those 1830s guitars, is still a mightily important presence in the flat-top market. Martin's

◄ **TAYLOR 814CE**

PRODUCED: *c1985-current*

THIS EXAMPLE: *2000*

BODY: *15¾" wide, 4⅝" deep*

This is Taylor's prime cutaway model, a great success that has done much to put the modern California-based Taylor operation on the guitar map. (The C of the model name indicates cutaway; the E is for electric, hence the controls seen on the side of the body.) A wide variety of players are drawn to the Taylor sound and playability, with 814CE guitarists including in recent years the great punk poet Patti Smith.

◄ **COLLINGS D-2H**

PRODUCED: *c1981-current*

THIS EXAMPLE: *2001*

BODY: *15¾" wide, 4¾" deep*

This model is one of Collings's renowned Martin-inspired Dreadnought-shaped acoustics, which explains the "D" prefix to the model. The instrument employs an East Indian rosewood back and sides and spruce top, with "pre-war" style scalloped internal bracing, to maximize the vibration of the guitar's top. A fine visual touch is Collings's traditional diamond fingerboard inlays.

▲ **SANTA CRUZ MODEL D**

PRODUCED: *1980-current*

THIS EXAMPLE: *1999*

BODY: *15½" wide, 4⅝" deep*

Richard Hoover started his career as an instrument maker building guitars and mandolins in 1972, but by 1976 had found his true calling, making fine, steel-strung, flat-top acoustics. The Model D, for example, offers a balanced tonal spectrum rather than this design's traditional bassiness. Santa Cruz players include Joan Baez, Elvis Costello, and Janis Ian – a respected songwriter but sadly underrated as a guitar-player.

instruments range across a wider price spectrum than ever, while the high-end models are still well regarded by leading players and have maintained a place on the tour-bus and in the studio with many of them.

The two primary rivals for Martin approach the market from opposite corners. Bill Collings, whom we have already met in the Blue Guitar Collection (p.121), began to make flat-tops in 1973, at first in Houston and then a few years later in Austin, Texas, where he is still based today. Starting as a small one-man shop with the highest attention to detail and personal service, Collings gained a glowing reputation for his instruments, most notably the deluxe flat-tops strongly influenced by 1930s Martins, but also some fine archtop guitars. Gradually the flat-tops have taken precedence, and

Collings has employed a number of additional workers. But the principal attraction of quality and excellence remains in the current output of the Collings operation. The company's work-rate is satisfyingly slow; between the beginning of 1999 and the first few months of 2001 some 1,800 instruments left the Collings workshop.

Bob Taylor and Kurt Listug set up in the guitar business in California in 1974. Today, based in El Cajon where the company has been since 1992, Taylor Guitars is a remarkable success, with Taylor and Listug still at the helm of a company which grows in stature and output year by year.

When the company started in the 1970s, Taylor's main competition came from other fine, smaller makers such as Mossman and Gurian, but today they are taking on no less a

► MARTIN OM-42

PRODUCED: *1930, 1999-current*

THIS EXAMPLE: *2000*

BODY: *15⅛" wide, 4" deep*

Martin's OM, or Orchestra Model, first appeared back in the early 1930s, as we've already discovered (see p.45). This was the company's first "14-fret" model, inspired by a request from banjoist Perry Bechtel to make "a guitar that feels like a banjo". Martin's regular guitar design had the neck joining the body at the 12th fret. But the new guitar for Bechtel had a shorter body that left 14 frets clear – a design that has since become established as the finest ever for fingerstyle players.

▼ MARTIN BACKPACKER

PRODUCED: *1994-current*

THIS EXAMPLE: *2000*

BODY: *7⅞" wide, 2" deep*

This small "travel guitar" was designed by New Jersey maker Bob McNally to take on the road as a knockabout instrument for everyday use. Its popularity led Martin to produce it at its factory in Mexico which until 1994 had been used for string and pickup making. Astronaut Pierre Thuot took a Backpacker on a '94 Shuttle mission, strumming to the stars, and the petite box has been in bulk production ever since.

◄ LARRIVÉE CHERUB

PRODUCED: *c1998-current*

THIS EXAMPLE: *2001*

BODY: *13¼" wide, 3¾" deep*

This is Canadian maker Jean Larrivée's take on the Baby guitar idea. Larrivée started building guitars in the early 1970s, and by 1998 had moved to a large new facility in the heart of Vancouver.

▲ MINI-MARTIN LIMITED EDITION

PRODUCED: *2000*

THIS EXAMPLE: *2000*

BODY: *11¼" wide, 3⅞" deep*

After the success of its Backpacker (see above), Martin came up with this Baby-style guitar, a modern version of the company's old Style 5 "Parlor" or "Terz" guitars, and developed by Martin's Dick Boak.

▶ **MARTIN HD-28LSV**

PRODUCED: *1997-current*

THIS EXAMPLE: *1999*

BODY: *15⅝" wide, 4¾" deep*

Part of the attraction of Martin's Style 28 instruments had been the distinctive herringbone trim, dropped after World War II. That and the sound-enhancing "scalloped braces" were reinstated in 1976. This recent version of the revitalized D-28 has an unusual large soundhole, and is modeled on the guitar used by the great bluegrass player Clarence White. It is part of Martin's new and successful Vintage series.

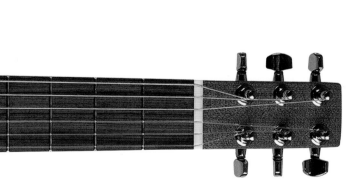

◀ **COLLINGS BABY**

PRODUCED: *c1998-current*

THIS EXAMPLE: *1999*

BODY: *12⅝" wide, 3¾" deep*

Texan maker Bill Collings also had a stab at the scaled-down Baby style of flat-top, exemplified by this recent example. The aim is a practical and perfectly acceptable sonic result in a physically reduced package.

rival than Martin – and making a real impact. An early success was a suitably purple-stained 655 12-string model built for Prince in the mid 1980s – but as the great man would not be seen using an instrument with a visible brandname, Taylor lost the immediate visual bonus associated with a guitar that went on to be seen in several Prince videos and a number of key performances. But the company more than made up for it by telling everyone they knew. Gradually, more players have become aware of Taylor and their fine, respected guitars.

At the close of the 1980s, Taylor invested heavily in computer-controlled machinery, one of the key factors in the company's subsequent growth. The physical statistics of Taylor's operation during the first year of the 21st century tells its own story of this development: some 330 staff, more than 85,000 square feet of production and office space, and over 35,000 instruments shipped each year. Taylor players are to be found in all kinds of music, from slide wizard Bonnie Raitt to the boisterous Billy Corgan, ex-Smashing Pumpkins.

Taylor has also been associated with the popularity of the scaled-down Baby guitar, an item that suits traveling musicians who are looking for a conveniently sized guitar to drag around on tour or to their favorite secluded writing location. The company opened a new factory extension in 2000 specially to cater for demand. So it is that acoustic guitarists in recent years seem just as likely to pick on a tiny Baby as on a big, bassy Dreadnought-style box.

▲ **TAYLOR BABY**

PRODUCED: *1996-current*

THIS EXAMPLE: *2001*

BODY: *11½" wide, 3¾" deep*

Taylor's fine Baby models come with a number of timber options, including koa, mahogany, maple and rosewood backs, as well as the gorgeous figured bubinga of this example (see the back, above). Tops are generally spruce, as here, but there is an all-mahogany version available of the little wonder.

► **GUILD F50R-NT**

PRODUCED: *1954-1987*

THIS EXAMPLE: *1975*

BODY: *17" wide, 5" deep*

Guild have always been noted for fine flat-tops like this one. The future of the company seemed secure when Fender bought Guild in 1995.

▼ **FENDER LEO FENDER BROADCASTER**

PRODUCED: *2000*

THIS EXAMPLE: *2000*

BODY: *12 ¼" wide, 1 ⅞" deep*

This limited-edition Custom Shop model from Fender celebrated the 50th anniversary of the world's first commercial solidbody electric guitar, marking a momentous occasion in guitar history. It is also notable as the only Fender guitar to have included on the headstock the forename of the company's founder as well as the more familiar surname.

2000

*FENDER HONORS FOUNDER
WITH ANNIVERSARY
BROADCASTER MODEL*

Fender and Gibson, the two key names in the development of the electric guitar, are significant 21st-century survivors.

The retro craze had a marked effect on the activity of the two most famous guitar brandnames, Fender and Gibson. Both had tried over the years to introduce new models that reflect and in some cases lead the contemporary advances in technical design and construction. And as we have seen throughout this book, many new brands have been coming along especially in the last few decades to rival and often overtake the achievements and popularity of the Big Two.

Yet Fender and Gibson have suffered from players expecting them to "make guitars the way they used to make them." How well situated they were, then, to exploit the retro trend and to make their old designs – and make them better than anyone else. As the 1990s progressed it became clear that both companies, while still able and willing to innovate, began to realize the tremendous value of their past achievements. New series of reissue instruments began to

▼ FENDER TORONADO

PRODUCED: *1998-current*

THIS EXAMPLE: *1998*

BODY: *12 ½" wide, 1 ¼" deep*

Fender started in the U.S., but by the 1990s was using a variety of worldwide sources, including its Mexico factory where this was made.

▲ FENDER JAG-STANG

PRODUCED: *1996-1998*

THIS EXAMPLE: *1997*

BODY: *11" wide, 1 ¾" deep*

Another overseas product for Fender was this Japanese-made Jag-Stang, launched in 1996. Left-hander Kurt Cobain of key grunge band Nirvana often used an old Fender Mustang on-stage. Cobain merged the look of his Mustang with some of the design features of a Fender Jaguar he also occasionally used and came up with the hybrid style of the Jag-Stang, an example of which was custom-built for him by Fender's Custom Shop. After Cobain's untimely death in 1994 his family collaborated with Fender to release the production version shown here.

▼ GIBSON HISTORIC COLLECTION FIREBIRD VII

PRODUCED: *1999-current*

THIS EXAMPLE: *1999*

BODY: *13" wide, 1 ¼" deep*

Gibson had recognized the value of reissuing its most famous designs for some years, but in 1993 renamed and reorganized the program as the Historic Collection. The new series stepped forwards and backwards at the time, using old specifications, but made with modern production methods. This fabulous Firebird is a perfect example of Gibson's new-found confidence.

▲ GIBSON LES PAUL DC STANDARD

PRODUCED: *1998-1999*

THIS EXAMPLE: *1998*

The revered Les Paul series has not been left entirely alone by Gibson in

recent years. Perhaps the company saw the success that PRS was having with a strongly Gibson-influenced double-cutaway design, and added another cutaway to its own best-known solidbody model, thus creating the DC.

▼ GIBSON 60s DOVE

PRODUCED: *1997-current*

THIS EXAMPLE: *Sep. 1998*

BODY: *16" wide, 4⅝" deep*

Gibson's great flat-tops also benefited from the reissue program, not least the Dove model which had first been issued in the early 1960s.

appear, with an increasing emphasis on exacting recreations of almost all of the two brands' especially hallowed models from earlier decades.

In 2000, Fender issued a remarkable tribute to its founder, Leo Fender. The Broadcaster model, introduced in 1950, was the original incarnation of the company's first solidbody electric guitar, a uniquely important instrument in guitar history, and a true mark of Leo Fender's brilliance. The Leo Fender Broadcaster came in a limited edition of just 50, and marked the 50th anniversary of the world's first commercial solidbody electric guitar. Somewhere, Leo Fender and Orville Gibson may have raised a glass of something special. To the future – and to more great guitars.

GLOSSARY

Alternative terms are shown (in brackets) following the key word.

acoustic General term for any hollowbody acoustic guitar. An acoustic musical instrument is one that generates sound without electrical amplification. Also, a term related to sound or hearing action

action Often used to describe just the height of the strings above the tops of the frets; thus "high action," "low action," "buzz-free action" etc. In fact, action refers to the entire playing feel of a given instrument; thus "good action," "easy action" etc.

active (active electronics, active circuit) Circuit in some guitars that boosts signal and/or widens tonal range with necessary additional (usually battery) powering. Refers to a pickup or circuit that incorporates a pre-amp. See pre-amp.

Alnico Magnet material used for pickups: an alloy of aluminum, nickel, and cobalt. Nickname for Gibson pickup with flat-sided polepieces.

amplifier Electrical circuit designed to increase a signal; usually, an audio system for boosting sound before transmission to a loudspeaker.

analog A system which reproduces a signal by copying its original amplitude waveform. Examples include the groove of an old vinyl recording, the electrical signal on a magnetic tape recording, or the voltage levels of an analog synthesizer. As opposed to digital, where the signal is recorded as a series of numbers.

anodized Finish given to metal by electrolysis. Often refers to Fender's gold-tinted aluminum pickguards of the 1950s.

archtop Guitar with arched body top formed by carving or pressing. Usually refers to hollowbody or semi-acoustic instruments; thus "archtop jazz guitar."

backline Amplifiers and speakers used for on-stage sound.

backplate Panel fitted over cavity in rear of guitar body, allowing access to pots and wiring or vibrato springs.

Bakelite The first plastic (invented 1909) and used for some guitars from the 1930s to the 1950s.

ball-end Metal retainer wound on to the end of a guitar string and used to secure it to the anchor point at the bridge.

Bigsby Almost generic term for a simple, single-spring, non-recessed vibrato system. Developed by Paul Bigsby.

binding Protective and decorative strip(s) added to edges of the body and/or fingerboard and/or headstock of some guitars.

blade pickup (bar pickup) Pickup (humbucker or single-coil) that uses a long single blade-polepiece per coil, rather than individual polepieces per string.

block markers Square-shape or rectangular-shape fingerboard position markers.

blond (blonde) Natural finish, usually enhancing plain wood color; or (on some Fenders) slightly yellowed finish.

bobbin Frame around which pickup coils are wound.

body The main portion of the guitar, on to which are (usually) mounted the bridge, pickups, controls etc. Can be solid, hollow, or a combination of the two.

bolt-on-neck Neck-to-body joint popularized by Fender – and actually most often secured by screws.

bookmatched Wood split into two thin sheets and joined to give symmetrically matching grain patterns.

bound See binding.

bout Looking at a guitar standing upright, the bouts are the outward curves of the body above (upper bout) and below (lower bout) the instrument's waist.

bracing Series of wooden struts inside hollowbody guitar providing strength and affecting tone.

bridge Unit on guitar body that holds the saddle(s). Sometimes also incorporates the anchor point for the strings.

bridge pickup Pickup placed nearest the bridge.

bridgeplate Baseplate on to which bridge components are mounted.

bullet Describes appearance of truss-rod adjustment nut at headstock on some Fender-style guitars.

capo (capo tasto, capo dastro) Movable device which can be fitted over the fingerboard behind any given fret, shortening the string length and therefore raising the strings' pitches.

cavity Hollowed-out area in solidbody guitar for controls and switches: thus "control cavity."

center block Solid wooden block running through the inside of a true semi-acoustic guitar's body.

chamfer Bevel or slope to body edges.

coil(s) Insulated wire wound around bobbin(s) in a pickup.

coil-split Usually describes a method to cut out one coil of a humbucking pickup giving a slightly lower output and a cleaner, more single-coil-like sound. Also known, incorrectly, as coil-tap.

coil-tap (tapped pickup) Pickup coil which has two or more live leads exiting at different percentages of the total wind in order to provide multiple output levels and tones. Not to be confused with coil-split.

combo Combination amplifier/speaker system in one unit.

contoured body Gentle curving of solid guitar body, aiding player comfort.

control cavity Hollowed-out area in solidbody guitar's body for controls, pickups and so on.

control(s) Knobs and switch levers on outside of guitar activating the function of electric components that are usually mounted behind the pickguard or in a body cavity.

course Usually means a pair of strings running together but tuned apart, usually in unison or an octave apart, as on a 12-string guitar. Technically, can also refer to a single string (or, rarely, a group of three strings).

custom color A selected color finish for a guitar, as opposed to natural or sunburst. Term originated by Fender in the late 1950s, now widely used.

cutaway Curve into body near neck joint, aiding player's access to high frets. A guitar can have two ("double," "equal," "offset") cutaways or one ("single") cutaway. Sharp (Gibson's "florentine") or round (Gibson's "venetian") describe the shape of the horn formed by the cutaway.

digital A system which stores and processes analog information by converting it into a series of numbers.

dings Small knocks, dents or other signs of normal wear in a guitar's surface. A true indicator of aged beauty if you're selling; a cause for mirth and money-saving if you're buying.

distortion Signal degradation caused by the overloading of audio systems. Often used deliberately to create a harsher, grittier sound.

dive-bomb See down-bend.

dog-ear Nickname for some P-90 pickups, derived from the shape of the mounting lugs on cover. See also soap-bar.

dot markers Dot-shape position markers on fingerboard.

dot-neck Fingerboard with dot-shape position markers; nickname for Gibson ES-335 of 1958-62 with such markers.

double-neck Large guitar specially made with two necks, usually combining six-string and 12-string, or six-string and bass.

down-bend Downward shift in the strings' pitch using a vibrato. In extreme cases this is known as "dive-bombing."

droopy headstock (pointy headstock) Long, down-pointing headstock popularized on 1980s superstrats.

effects Generic term for audio processing devices such as distortions, delays, reverbs, flangers, phasers, harmonizers and so on.

electric A term simply applied to any electric guitar (in other words one used in conjunction with an amplifier).

electro-acoustic (electro) Acoustic guitar with built-in pickup, usually of piezo-electric type. The guitar usually has a built-in pre-amp including volume and tone controls. For the purposes of this book, such a guitar is not considered to be an electric guitar. (To qualify, it must have at least one magnetic pickup.)

equalization (EQ) Active tone control that works by emphasizing or de-emphasizing specific frequency bands.

feedback Howling noise produced by leakage of the output of an amplification system back into its input, typically a guitar's pickup(s).

f-hole Soundhole of approximately "f" shape on some hollowbody and semi-acoustic guitars.

figure Pattern on surface of wood; thus "figured maple" and so on.

fine-tuners Set of tuners that tune strings to very fine degrees, usually as fitted to a locking vibrato or bridge.

fingerboard (fretboard, board) Playing surface of the guitar that holds the frets. It can be simply the front of the neck itself, or a separate thin board glued to the neck.

finish Protective and decorative covering, often paint, on wood parts, typically the guitar's body, back of neck, and headstock.

fixed bridge Non-vibrato bridge.

flame Dramatic figure, usually on maple.

flat-top Acoustic with flat top (in other words, not arched) and usually with a round soundhole.

floating bridge Bridge not fixed permanently to the guitar's top, but held in place by string tension (usually on older or old-style hollowbody guitars).

floating pickup Pickup not fixed permanently to the guitar's top, but mounted on a separate pickguard or to the end of the fingerboard (on some hollowbody electric guitars).

floating vibrato Vibrato unit (such as the Floyd Rose or Wilkinson type) that "floats" above the surface of the body.

frequency The number of cycles of a carrier wave per second; the perceived pitch of a sound.

fretless Guitar fingerboard without frets; usually bass, but sometimes (very rarely) guitar.

frets Metal strips positioned on the fingerboard of a guitar (or sometimes directly into the face of the solid neck) to enable the player to stop the strings and produce specific notes.

fretboard See fingerboard.

fretwire Wire from which individual frets are cut.

glued neck See set-neck.

hang-tag Small cards and other documents hung on to a guitar in the showroom.

hardtail Guitar (originally Fender Strat-style) with non-vibrato bridge.

hardware Any separate components (non-electrical) fitted to the guitar: bridge, tuners, strap buttons and so on.

headless Design with no headstock, popularized by Ned Steinberger in the early 1980s.

headstock Portion at the end of the neck where the strings attach to the tuners. "Six-tuners-in-line" type (Fender-style) has all six tuners on one side of the headstock. "Three-tuners-a-side" type (Gibson-style) has three tuners on one side and three the other.

heel Curved deepening of the neck for strength near body joint.

hex pickup Provides suitable signal for synthesizer.

high-end (up-market, upscale) High- or higher-cost instrument, usually aimed at those seeking the best quality, materials and workmanship.

horn Pointed body shape formed by cutaway: thus left horn, right horn. See also cutaway.

humbucker Noise-canceling twin-coil pickup. Typically the two coils have opposite magnetic polarity and are wired together electrically out-of-phase to produce a sound that we call in-phase.

hybrid Technically, any instrument that combines two systems of any kind, but now used to indicate a guitar that combines original-style magnetic "electric" pickups with "acoustic"-sounding piezo pickups.

inlay Decorative material cut and fitted into body, fingerboard, headstock etc.

intonation State of a guitar so that it is as in-tune with itself as physically possible. This is usually dependent on setting the string's speaking length by adjusting the point at which the strings cross the bridge saddle, known as intonation adjustment. Some bridges allow more adjustment, and therefore greater possibilities for accurate intonation, than others.

jack (jack socket) Mono or stereo connecting socket used to feed guitar's output signal to amplification.

jackplate Mounting plate for output jack (jack socket), usually screwed on to body.

laminated Joined together in layers; usually wood (bodies, necks) or plastic (pickguards).

locking nut Unit that locks strings in place at the nut, usually with three locking bolts.

locking trem See locking vibrato.

locking tuner Special tuner that locks the string to the string-post and thus aids string-loading.

locking vibrato Type of vibrato system that locks strings at nut and saddles (hence also called "double-locking") to stabilize tuning.

logo A brandname or trademark, usually on headstock.

low-end (bargain, down-market) Low- or lower-cost instrument, often aimed at beginners or other players on a budget.

lower bout See bout.

luthier Fancy name for guitar maker.

machine head See tuner.

GLOSSARY

magnetic pickup Transducer using coils of wire wound around a magnet. It converts string vibrations into electrical signals.

master volume/tone Control that affects all pickups equally.

MIDI Musical Instrument Digital Interface. The industry-standard control system for electronic instruments. Data for notes, performance effects, patch changes, voice and sample data, tempo and other information can be transmitted and received.

mod Short for modification; any change made to a guitar.

mother-of-pearl (pearl) Lustrous internal shell of some molluscs, eg abalone, used for inlay. Synthetic "pearloid" versions exist.

mounting ring Usually plastic unit within which Gibson-style pickups are fitted to the guitar body.

neck Part of the guitar supporting the fingerboard and strings; glued or bolted to the body, or on "though-neck" types forming a support spine on to which "wings" are usually glued to form the body.

neck pitch Angle of a guitar's neck relative to the body face.

neckplate Single metal plate through which screws pass to achieve bolt-on neck (Fender-style).

neck pickup Pickup placed nearest the neck.

neck-tilt Device on some Fender (and other) neck-to-body joints allowing easier adjustment of neck pitch.

noise Any undesirable sound, such as mains hum or interference.

noise-canceling Type of pickup with two coils wired together to cancel noise, often called humbucking. Any arrangement of pickups or pickup coils that achieves this.

nut Bone, metal or (now usually) synthetic slotted guide bar over which the strings pass to reach the tuners and which determines string height and spacing at the headstock end of neck.

nut lock See locking nut.

offshore Made overseas; and more specifically often used to mean outside the US.

PAF Gibson pickup with Patent Applied For decal on base.

passive Normal, unboosted circuit.

pearl See mother-of-pearl.

pearloid Fake pearl, made of plastic and pearl dust.

pickup See transducer.

piezo pickup (piezo-electric pickup) Transducer with piezo-electric crystals that generate electricity under mechanical strain – in a guitar, it senses string and body movement. "Piezo-loaded saddles" are bridge saddles with an integral piezo element.

pickguard (scratchplate) Protective panel fitted flush on to body, or raised above body.

pickup switch (pickup selector) Selector switch that specifically selects pickups individually or in combination.

pitch The perceived "lowness" or "highness" of a sound, determined by its frequency.

plectrum (flat pick) Small piece of (usually) plastic or metal used to pluck or strum a guitar's strings.

P-90 Early Gibson single-coil pickup.

pointy A type of body design prevalent in the 1980s and since with a jagged, pointed, angular outline.

pointy headstock See droopy headstock.

polepieces Non-magnetic (but magnetically conductive) polepieces are used to control, concentrate and/or shape the pickup's magnetic field. Can be either adjustable (screw) or non-adjustable (slug), as in an original Gibson humbucker. Magnetic polepieces are those where the magnet itself is aimed directly at the strings, as in an original Stratocaster single-coil.

position markers (fingerboard markers) Fingerboard inlays of various designs used as a guide for fret positions.

pot (potentiometer) Variable electrical resistor that alters voltage by a spindle turning on an electrically resistive track. Used for volume and tone controls, and so on.

pre-amp (pre-amplifier) Guitar circuit, usually powered by a battery, that converts the pickup's output from high to low impedance (pre-amp/buffer) and can increase the output signal and boost or cut specific frequencies for tonal effect.

pre-CBS Fender guitars made before CBS takeover in 1965.

pressed top Arched top (usually laminated) of hollowbody guitar made by machine-pressing rather than hand-carving.

purfling Usually synonymous with binding, but more accurately refers to the decorative inlays around the perimeter of a guitar alongside the binding.

quilted Undulating figure, usually on maple.

radius Slight curve, or camber, of a fingerboard surface, the strings, or the bridge saddles.

refinished (refin) New finish added, replacing or over the original.

resonator Generic term for guitar with metal resonator in body to increase volume.

retro A past style reintroduced, often with some changes, as a "new" design, usually with deliberate references. Thus retro guitars use flavors of mainly 1950s and 1960s designs to inform new designs.

retrofit Any component (pickup, vibrato, tuner and so on) added to a guitar after it leaves the place where it was made that fits directly on to the intended guitar with no alteration to the instrument.

reverb (reverberation) Ambience effect combining many short echoes; can be imitated electronically.

rout Hole or cavity cut into a guitar, usually into the body. Such cavities are said to be routed into the body.

saddle(s) Part(s) of a bridge where the strings make contact; the start of the speaking length of the string, effectively the opposite of the nut.

scale length (string length) Theoretical length of the vibrating string from nut to saddle; actually twice the distance from nut to 12th fret. The actual scale length (the distance from the nut to saddle after intonation adjustment) is slightly longer. See intonation.

selector Control that selects from options, usually of pickups.

semi See semi-acoustic.

semi-acoustic (semi-solid, semi) Electric guitar with wholly or partly hollow body. Originally used specifically to refer to an electric guitar with a solid wooden block running down the center of a thinline body, such as Gibson's ES-335.

semi-solid See semi-acoustic.

serial number Added by maker for own purposes; sometimes useful for determining construction and/or shipping date.

set-neck (glued neck, glued-in neck, fixed neck) Type of neck/body joint popularized by Gibson which permanently "sets" the two main components together, usually by gluing.

INDEX

BIBLIOGRAPHY & THANKS

BIBLIOGRAPHY

Charles Alexander (ed) Masters Of Jazz Guitar (Miller Freeman 1999); **Tony Bacon** Fifty Years Of Fender (Miller Freeman 2000), Electric Guitars: The Illustrated Encyclopedia (Thunder Bay/Balafon 2000); **Tony Bacon** (ed) Echo & Twang (Backbeat 2001), Fuzz & Feedback (Miller Freeman 2000); **Tony Bacon & Paul Day** The Fender Book (Miller Freeman 1998), The Gibson Les Paul Book (Miller Freeman 1993), The Gretsch Book (Miller Freeman 1996), The Rickenbacker Book (Miller Freeman 1994), The Ultimate Guitar Book (DK 1991); **Tony Bacon & Barry Moorhouse** The Bass Book (Miller Freeman 1995); **Bob Brozman** The History & Artistry of National Resonator Instruments (Centerstream 1993); **Walter Carter** Epiphone: The Complete History (Hal Leonard 1995), Gibson: 100 Years Of An American Icon (General Publishing 1994), The Martin Book (Miller Freeman 1995); **A.R. Duchossoir** Gibson Electrics - The Classic Years (Hal Leonard 1994); **Tom & Mary Anne Evans** Guitars: Music, History, Construction And Players (Oxford University Press 1977); **Hugh Gregory** 1000 Great Guitarists (Miller Freeman 1994); **George Gruhn & Walter Carter** Acoustic Guitars (GPI 1993), Electric Guitars And Basses (GPI 1994), Gruhn's Guide To Vintage Guitars (Miller Freeman 1999); **Robert Carl Hartman** Guitars And Mandolins In America, featuring the Larsons' Creations (Maurer 1988); **Steve Howe & Tony Bacon** The Steve Howe Guitar Collection (IMP/Miller Freeman 1994); **JTG** Gibson Shipping Totals 1946-1979 (JTG 1992); **Barry Kernfeld** (ed) The New Grove Dictionary Of Jazz (Macmillan 1994); **Colin Larkin** (ed) The Guinness Encyclopedia Of Popular Music four volumes (Guinness 1992); **Mike Longworth** Martin Guitars: A History (Four Maples 1988); **John Morrish** The Fender Amp Book (Miller Freeman 1995); **Pete Prown & HP Newquist** Legends Of Rock Guitar

(Hal Leonard 1997); **Stanley Sadie** (ed) The New Grove Dictionary of Musical Instruments three volumes (Macmillan 1984); **Paul William Schmidt** Acquired Of The Angels: D'Angelico & D'Aquisto (Scarecrow 1991); **Jay Scott** 50s Cool: Kay Guitars (Seventh String Press 1992); **Richard R Smith** Fender: The Sound Heard Round The World (Garfish 1995); **John Teagle** Washburn (Music Sales 1996); **Akira Tsumura** Guitars – The Tsumura Collection (Kodansha 1987); **Thomas A Van Hoose** The Gibson Super 400 (GPI 1991); **René Vannes** Dictionnaire Universel des Luthiers (Les Amis de la musique 1988); **Tom Wheeler** American Guitars (HarperPerennial 1990); **Joel Whitburn** Pop Memories 1890-1954 (Record Research 1986); **Eldon Whitford** et al Gibson's Fabulous Flat-Top Guitars (Miller Freeman 1994).

We also found various back issues of the following magazines helpful: Acoustic Guitar; Guitar Player; Guitar Magazine (UK); The Music Trades; Vintage Gallery; Vintage Guitar; 20th Century Guitar; Wood & Steel. A number of manufacturers' websites provided some useful information.

THANKS

The author and publishers would like to thank: the late Scott Chinery; Julie Bowie; Mike Carey; Walter Carter; Doug Chandler; François Charle; Grant Collins (Acoustic Centre, London); Paul Day; Pat Foley (Gibson London); Ted Garner; Michael Holmes; Steve Howe; Dave Hunter (Guitar Magazine); Mikael Jansson; Ira B. Kraemer; Neville Marten (Guitarist); Barry Moorhouse (Acoustic Centre, London); Mike Newton; Jim Noble (for the photograph of PRS Singlecut p.133); Marc Quigley (PRS Guitars); Miki Slingsby; Steve Soest (Soest Guitar Repair); Sally Stockwell; Michael Wright.